THE
HEALING
TOUCH
OF
MARY

DIVINE IMPRESSIONS
27 Long Spur
Littleton, CO 80127
800.682.1729

Printed in South Korea.

Library of Congress Control Number: 2005902214

ISBN 0-9767164-9-6

The Healing Touch of Mary is dedicated to my earthly mother who was my biggest challenge and to my Divine Mother who loves me unconditionally.

• CONTENTS •

· FOREWORD ·

When I opened this lovely and inspiring book, Cheri Lomonte's exquisite photographs of Mary provoked a visceral memory of the faith of my childhood.

Mary was a constant, visible presence in my home, my grandparents' home, friends' homes…at school and, of course, at church. She was represented by rosaries, novena books, holy cards, medals, statues, pastel figurines and, most of all, pictures. She reigned as the compassionate, understanding guardian and protector to whom we addressed our daily prayers. God, all-knowing but mysteriously unknowable, seemed frightening, forbidding, and perhaps too busy with important things to bother with a child's concerns. Mary, on the other hand, seemed immanently knowable, an easily accessible mother who understood us and always had time for us.

As I grew older, the Mary of my childhood prayers receded in my imagination like the blue fairy in Pinocchio for whom I mistook her when I first saw the Disney film. In the all-male high school and college I attended, devotion to Jesus replaced Mary at the center of our prayers. Mary was held up to us as a vigilant guardian of our purity. "Don't disappoint her," we were admonished. "Don't contribute to her suffering!" Otherwise, she was largely consigned to the role of model for good Christian women, obedient, loyal, long-suffering and silent.

Too frequently, she is still relegated to this limited role. If this is all there is to Mary, how has she managed to sustain her place in the hearts and imaginations of both the doubting and the faithful? What accounts for our continued attraction to her, generation after generation?

Revisionist scholars suggest that Mary's popularity over the centuries is due to the fact that she is a thinly veiled symbol of our desire for "goddess worship," which has been suppressed by patriarchy. While there is evidence that the church in some cultures has appropriated qualities of goddesses and attributed them to Mary, this alone cannot account for the abiding devotion people have to her. A goddess is by nature aloof and distant. Immediacy and accessibility are essential to Mary's appeal.

Sentimentalizing, idealizing, or deifying Mary robs her of both her humanity and her faith. And it is, I believe, the wonderful fullness of her humanity and faith that inspires us and draws us to her as indeed it drew God.

In a "new age" that too easily confuses self-obsession with self-esteem, Mary challenges us as an unparalleled role model of authentic self-esteem. Mary's self-esteem is relational growing out of her understanding of who she is in relationship to God. Paradoxically, it is her complete humility, her absolute reliance on God that gives her her self-esteem. In this, she perfectly embodies the idea expressed by Isak Dinesen in her great novel, Out of Africa, "Pride is faith in the idea that God had when He made us."

Her faith in herself as God's creature allows her to fully embrace and mirror God's faith in her. It is this faith that gives her the self-esteem to respond to God with an unhesitating, existential, "Yes!" Her "Be it done unto me according to thy will," prefigures and births Jesus' "Thy will be done."

It is the mystery, unfathomable to most of us, of her capacity for spontaneous surrender—to move without calculation or reservation into union with Divine Will—that so inspires and challenges us. We almost can't quite bear for her to be human. If we allow her to be fully human she robs us of our "Nos," our "Maybes" and—most of all—our "Impossibles."

The stories in this inspiring book are filled with the testimonies of people who dared to pray to Mary and surrender to her their "Impossibles"—situations they believed could only be healed by the miraculous.

Perhaps the reason we pray to Mary, trust Mary to go to God for us is because we cannot imagine her saying "No." And how could God say "No" to her when it never occurred to her to say "No" to God?

Jim Curtan, Faculty Member,
The Caroline Myss Education Institute

· AUTHOR'S NOTE ·

Thousands of titles and names are attributed to Mary. Don't be confused—the different names do not pertain to different individuals. You will find Mary, Mother of God, with a title of Our Lady of Guadalupe, La Conquistadora, Our Blessed Mother, Our Lady of Fatima, Our Lady of Virtues and Gospa.

It's a matter of history, culture and location how her different names were given and how she was identified. For example, during the 1870s in France, Mary was given the title Our Lady of Hope due to the war that was taking place between France and Germany.

I have received permission to print the following stories, poems and prayers. Occasionally the names of friends or relatives were changed to protect their privacy. Two of the stories were told to me asking for anonymity. I agreed to that.

You will find some small caveats identified by the person's initials and, in most cases, the state where they are from. Those stories came from the Lourdes Center in Boston. The Center was kind enough to give me permission to use these stories.

The book is printed as a non-profit endeavor. The profits will be distributed to, but not limited to, La Confradia in Santa Fe, New Mexico, and the Boston Lourdes Center, Boston, Massachusetts.

Cheri Lomonte

THE
HEALING
TOUCH

OF MARY

CHERI LOMONTE

2

It was in the spring of 2002 and I was doing research for my final project before graduation when I found it. I have always had a special devotion to Our Lady, so when I found the beautiful bookmark of Our Lady of Guadalupe in the law book, I was thrilled. I remember feeling very lucky for my find.

I also remember feeling very lucky again when my blood work from my annual physical exam came back "perfect." I was healthy and ready to finish my degree and concentrate on my daughter's summer wedding. And that is exactly what I did.

But after the wedding, I began to notice something was not right. I felt tired and overwhelmed by the slightest things. And that bookmark kept popping into my mind for no apparent reason.

I decided to go back to my doctor, and this time I asked to see the complete report from my annual physical. And what I saw shocked me.

My urinalysis was off, and my white blood count was high. The doctors had not been concerned, they said, because my numbers had only been "very slightly off." But I persisted, to my surprise. I am normally not one to push, but

3

something kept gnawing at me. And again the bookmark of Our Lady of Guadalupe kept resurfacing in my mind.

I asked my doctor for a referral to see a urologist, and after much persuasion, he agreed. He again insisted that I was fine, but if it would make me feel better, he thought I should see Dr. Vistro.

The CAT scan showed a mass on my ovary. And further tests showed it was cancer.

The first thing I did when I got home that day was find the bookmark and place it on my nightstand. Every night for the next six months as I went through a hysterectomy and then chemotherapy, I prayed. I prayed to Our Lady and I cherished the bookmark. I knew that there had to be a connection.

A few weeks after my last treatment, as I dropped in to see my department chair, an amazing thing happened. Her door was open but she was nowhere in sight. I figured that she would be right back so I sat down to wait for her. I was looking at the bookshelf behind her desk when my eyes wandered to the poster. I had been in Dr. Shevsky's office a million times, but I had never noticed the poster of Our Lady of Guadalupe, with the caption that said, "Our Lady, the window of health."

"Oh, my God," I said aloud, "how dumb can I be?"

That night, like every night since my first diagnosis, I reached for the bookmark on my nightstand. This time, however, I wanted to really look at her face and thank her for saving my life.

But the bookmark was gone.

That was almost two years ago, and I am still cancer free. I continue to thank Mary, Mother of God, for saving my life and, believe it or not, I continue to look for the bookmark of Our Lady of Guadalupe.

Liz P.

5

My husband was told in December that he had edema in the back of his left eye and there was a possibility of losing the eyesight in that eye. Every night he put Lourdes water on the outside of his eye and said the prayer to Our Lady of Lourdes. I did the novena every night. He just had another exam and the doctor said there is no edema.

T.P., Maine

6

There was nothing spoken, words seemed unnecessary as I gazed in amazement at the most beautiful face I had ever seen in my life. I remember thinking that I wanted always to be able to recall every detail of her divine face, but oddly enough, when I now try to describe it, I have no words, only the feeling of her divine presence. At the time, I didn't even question that this was happening to me—I allowed myself to feel the experience and accept the reality with peace and contentment.

I had just moved out of my parents' house when I saw this affirmation of my prayers, Mary, the Blessed Mother of God. My eyes opened and I remember focusing on her face. I couldn't believe that she was appearing to me, of all people, and in my bedroom. It all seemed so surreal and so unbelievable. Shouldn't Mary, Mother of God, be appearing at the Vatican or some holy shrine? What possible business did she have with me?

But soon I was to understand that perhaps she had chosen me as her messenger. My epiphany came a few months later when I was on my return from Italy. As we were preparing to land in New York City, a stranger approached me. She informed me that she had just returned

CHERI LOMONTE
A YOUNG MOTHER

from a pilgrimage to Medjugorje and felt that she needed to give me a picture of Mary. Her exact words, as I recall, were, "I feel strongly that I need to give you this picture." You can imagine my shock as the emerald eyes of this compelling woman held me captive while she told me how she had felt compelled to give me this picture. Of the five hundred passengers on board the plane, she had chosen me.

Normally I would have put the picture in my room at home, but for some reason I decided to frame it and place it in my work office. It sat on my desk for several years until one day a coworker approached me with a problem. He told me that he had always been drawn to the picture, but now he seemed to have a real connection. He informed me that he was worried about his wife. She had been visiting a home in Yonkers, where oil supposedly was seeping from a statue of the Blessed Mother. Honestly, I do believe the poor man thought his wife had lost her mind. Well, I told him that it could be true, and I would be happy to investigate for him.

On my way to Yonkers on that bright morning in April, I thought: why this place—Yonkers, near the Bronx? If this miracle was indeed true, shouldn't it be happening in Rome or Jerusalem? But as I arrived at the humble, freshly painted light blue house, I realized that, as usual, anything could happen. I would try to open my heart to the possibilities.

I arrived just before 7:00 a.m., a bit early for a Saturday, but I wanted to be sure that I had the right house and would have time to sit and think about the whole situation. But before I could even examine the house, a tiny, wrinkled woman with silvery hair and coal-colored eyes, approached my car, seemingly from out of nowhere. Her wide grin and quiet whisper assured me that she wasn't at all uncomfortable with me arriving at such an early hour. In fact, it almost seemed like she had been expecting me.

As I entered her home, I was taken aback by the dizzying scent. The woman seemed to know as she grabbed my arm and whispered something in my ear. I turned to her as if in a dream and realized she had said, "rose-scented." She motioned me toward a small room off of the kitchen, and as I approached I hesitated on the threshold as the scent overwhelmed my senses. I had never experienced anything like it in my entire life—it was sweet yet pungent, light yet powerful. I can still remember how the scent seemed to surround me like a fog, lingering above my head then flowing downward and around my body like a soft, comforting blanket.

And then I saw it. The statue of Mary was literally

oozing with oil. My first instinct was to walk around trying to find the pump or electrical connection. I remember thinking that this had to be some kind of hoax. But when I felt the oil, I knew that it was real. When you come in contact with the divine, you know…you just know. This was definitely real, and it was happening to me.

I made several visits to Muna's house after that. On one particular visit, Muna informed me that the oil had begun seeping from the walls and furniture as well as from the statue. She said she didn't know what to do about it, so she had begun using cotton to catch some of the oil. She also had begun giving away the cotton-soaked oil and offered me a bag. I accepted it, of course, brought home the precious gift, and placed it on my dresser. Little did I know that I soon would need to use this gift.

When I got the call several months later, I knew I had to go. I was afraid but I knew I had to do it. The baby was only three months old when she contracted meningitis and as I arrived at the hospital and saw all the long faces, I knew the prognosis was not a good one. In fact, I later found out that the sweet little cherub was not expected to live, but if she did, the doctor said, there would be severe damage. I talked to the family and every one of them was open to any prayers or any form of healing that might save their baby. I didn't know why or how I had come to be there or who in fact had known that I had the oil, but what I did know was that I had to use the oil for healing, and I had to do it now.

I walked into the immaculately white hospital room and saw the helpless child lying listlessly on the white linens, tubes emanating from what seemed like every part of her tiny body. I remember the very strange feeling that I knew exactly what to do. I walked over and touched her spine, gently rubbing the oil into her skin so as not to dislodge the tubes. She didn't move but I swear I saw a twitch of a smile as I continued to rub the oil up and down her spine. Two days later, little Eva was alert, nursing, and back in her family's arms. The doctor called it a miracle, and today Eva is perfectly fine.

From the silence of that first vision, from the lack of words and the awe, from the feeling of the divine presence, come the peace and the contentment in knowing that I have helped to bring joy and comfort to others. That I, an ordinary girl from New Jersey, have been given the gift of grace is still quite unbelievable to me, but I have accepted this calling. And when I am called again, I hope that I will hear and react accordingly, for if I have learned anything from this experience it is the old cliché—that it is truly in giving that you receive. And perhaps that is the true miracle.

Dawn J.

I want to share a story of a miracle that occurred with prayers and the healing water from Lourdes. One morning I received a call from my son, who lives next door to me, saying that my epileptic grandson was experiencing a "bad" seizure. I grabbed my bottle of Lourdes water and ran next door. My son was very concerned because my grandson was not breathing and the length of the seizure was approaching five minutes. I ran to the bed where Colin's lifeless body was lying, knelt down and poured the Lourdes water over his head and prayed to God and our blessed Mother for Colin to start breathing. After a minute, which seemed to go by as if it were an hour, he took a breath and let out a long sign. I am so grateful that my grandson's life was spared and so convinced of the power of the precious water of Lourdes.

E.M., Massachusetts

It was dark. I remember thinking that I could barely see my own hands in front of my face. But I really wasn't scared because I knew that I was among friends. My dear friend and coworker, Alice, sat to my left; my childhood friend, Kathleen, was to my right.

Then I felt hands on my shoulders. Soft, comforting hands moved from the center of my shoulders to the outside. I wanted to turn and look but I remember feeling like I didn't want to move because the hands felt so nice. I also remember how unusually warm my shoulders felt. It seemed as if the warmth came directly from the hands. I looked right and then left. Both Alice's and Kathleen's hands were clasped in prayer.

Then Alice turned to me and smiled. "Mary really loves you," she said. I was confused and my face told her so. "No, I mean, she really loves you," she continued. "Don't you feel it? She's holding you now."

I was stunned and confused and dared not move. Yes, I did feel the hands on my shoulders, but they felt human, not ethereal.

"Oh, my gosh, Jim." It was Kathleen who spoke this time. "You, you, have a … light all around you," she

14

stuttered in amazement.

And before I could even think, Alice closed her eyes and began to sing the Ave Maria in Italian. Kathleen and I just stared. Alice was from the heart of Nebraska, purebred American, had never been to Italy, and knew no Italian, whatsoever.

What was going on here? Was it some kind of trick? Do I dare turn to look? I had to move now, I remember thinking. So I did it. I turned my head to look behind me and immediately the feeling of warm hands on my shoulders disappeared, Alice stopped singing, and Kathleen whispered, "The light, Jim, the light has gone out." It all seemed to happen so fast.

And then we all looked at each other and knew. We didn't speak at that moment but we seemed to communicate with our eyes instead. And they said, yes, what we had experienced was real.

I had arrived at this Native American sweat lodge in southern Pennsylvania as Jim C., cancer patient and skeptic. I left the next day as Jim C., cancer patient and believer. I truly had no idea that Mary, Mother of God, would reveal herself to me on that cold November night. But I had felt her embrace, her warm hands on my cold shoulders.

15

I promised myself that I would never forget this night and always remember to praise Mary for her comfort.

That was November of 1999. Today I feel very fortunate that I am here to tell you that I believe in my heart that Mary's warm hands must have had something to do with the fact that today I am cancer free.

Jim C.

16

I had been experiencing gum pain around my teeth. When I went to visit the dentist he took x-rays and told me that I would probably need gum surgery and could very likely lose my two front teeth. He told me to return in a couple of weeks to begin the work. I went home and applied Lourdes water and prayed to Our Lady so I would not lose my teeth. When I returned to the dentist he said it was "phenomenal" and that my teeth were all okay for now. The problem had "disappeared"!

L.G., New York

I always greeted people after mass, shaking their hands and giving quick hugs or pats on the back. That has always been my way of connecting with the people…of letting them know that I am a real person and always available.

But this particular Sunday was different. People seemed to be looking at me funny. It was almost as if they wanted to tell me something but were too afraid. Yes, something was definitely odd. And it would take a tiny, precocious little girl to tell me.

I knew Kimmy Lou very well. In fact, I had baptized Kimmy seven years before, so when she reached into the basket for a Starburst candy, I grabbed her miniscule hand and kissed it. I was just about to greet Colin Russell, when I felt a tug on my robe.

"Father Michael, Father Michael," she said. "Are you sick today?"

"Why no, Kimmy, I feel just great," I said. "Why do you think that I'm sick? Do I look bad today?" I chuckled.

"Father, your hands are so hot," said Kimmy. "It's like they are on fire, Father."

I brought my hands together as I do in prayer. They were on fire, all right, burning like the burning bush in the Old

Testament. It all made sense. That is when I realized why people were looking at me funny. My first thoughts were that I must be sick. I would see a doctor tomorrow.

But Dr. Haslow said I was in perfect health. He had no idea why my hands were so hot, and getting hotter. He couldn't explain it and said that he had never seen anything like it.

I continued to live with my hot hands and prayed that they would get better. Meanwhile I also continued to give the Daily Mass for the Sick. That has always been my favorite mass, so I continued my services and tried not to think of my hands.

One day, though, three parishioners stopped me after the daily mass. They said that they had something to share with me. They each took turns telling me that their prayers had literally been answered. Frank Smith had prayed that his wife would be free of cancer. Yesterday's doctor visit unbelievably showed no signs of the vicious lung cancer she had been battling for nine months. Sadie Neely had prayed that her son, who had been out of work for a year, would find a job. Tuesday he had landed one of the biggest, most sought-after positions at Slifer and Sons law firm. And Donna Hunter had prayed that her sister's tumor was benign…and it was. All three agreed that I had been responsible for healing them.

Days and weeks passed and more people came to me to be healed. And to my surprise, more people were healed. I had never thought of being pastor as anything more than my duty, but I soon began to realize that God had assigned me another duty—the duty of healing.

Before I knew it, I had healed a man with the West Nile Virus, a woman with Parkinson's disease, and a child with leukemia.

To this day, I still possess the gift of healing, for I do believe that it is truly a gift from God. I accept it and cherish it, and can't quite explain it, except that perhaps God may be trying to reassure us that there is indeed goodness in these troubled times.

Father Michael W.

* Father Michael W. received his gift of healing in the early 1990s. He is pastor of St. Vincent de Paul church in Denver. He also started the Lourdes Marian Center there. The center is one of two locations in the United States where the healing water from Lourdes is available.

y name is Father David M., and I am a Canon Pastor in the Episcopalian church. Ever since I was a child, I have always had a special devotion to Mary, Mother of God. Because of this devotion, I truly believe that Mary calls me to help those in dire situations.

On one particular occasion, a close friend of mine, Susan, called me because her sister was very ill. When she asked that I visit her, I immediately agreed. In fact, I heard that voice again that seemed to say, "David, yes, go. Go, and now!"

I knew that Brenda had cancer and hepatitis, and I also knew her history. Brenda had always been the black sheep of the Stephens family. For years her siblings had tried to help her, but Brenda always seemed to be in trouble. When she was a teenager, she had experimented heavily with all types of drugs. In her twenties, she had several affairs with married men that got her in lots of trouble. When she announced that she was gay in her late thirties, her family was less than shocked. But they loved her dearly through it all.

I suppose I was the one shocked when I went to see Brenda. I had not seen her in many years, and what I saw then was a weak, suffering soul—a forty-one year old in an eighty-year-old body. Her skin was wrinkled and her eyes were glazed over. But her mind was solid.

"Father David," she smiled. "I am going to die soon, and I would like your blessing. As you know, I have not lived my life the way I should have. I have let down myself, my family, and my God."

I smiled too and assured her that God gives second and third and fourth chances. "All you have to do is remember that you once were a Christian and you can still gain your place in heaven by praying."

I was glad to see that Brenda still had a sense of humor because her immediate response was, "Father, my first prayer is that you come back tomorrow and visit me again."

Our second visit was nice. We talked about the family, and I noticed that Brenda had a certain twinkle in her eye that I had not noticed the day before. She told me that she had begun to pray as I had instructed and that although she did not know if it would do any good, she would continue to pray and ask forgiveness for her wasted life. And again she asked me to come back as soon as I could. I told her that the next day was Sunday, my busiest day of the week, so our next visit would probably have to be on Monday.

Sunday was a long, arduous day and when I finally was able to sit and rest, I found that I could not sit and rest. The voice was back. And the voice again said, "David, go now. Don't wait."

When I arrived at the hospital that night, I was surprised to find that Brenda had been moved to intensive care.

As I made my way down the long, white hall, I saw Susan sitting outside the door with her head in her hands. I touched her shoulder, and when she looked up at me, I saw the shock in her eyes.

"Oh, Father David, thank you so much for coming. But how did you know"?

"Well, I'm not quite sure, but can I see her?"

Susan told the nurse it was O.K., and as I made my way to Brenda's bed, I was very thankful that I had listened to that voice.

I sat and prayed and held her hand. I truly did not expect her to open her eyes, but when she did, I smiled and assured her that she would be fine. Brenda couldn't speak but she nodded her head and again closed her eyes.

"Brenda," I whispered. "I know that you can hear me. I want you to know that God loves you and if you pray as you did as a child—with an open heart—you will be welcomed into the kingdom of heaven. Don't be afraid. God is good and forgiving."

I watched as tears rolled from her closed eyes, and I sat with her for several hours.

And I prayed for her soul.

Brenda died that night. But she died in a state of grace because Mary, Mother of God called me to visit Brenda and to reconcile her to God. And hopefully I was able to do just that.

Father David M.

I had a stroke while walking to the bus to do my grocery shopping. I fell on the cement sidewalk and injured both knees (one very badly) and both wrists as I fell with much force. I could not walk and my knees were badly swollen. I applied some healing water from Lourdes and said prayers to Our Lady and the swelling went down. I live alone but walk daily. In a few days I was able to limp around. My knees and wrists are much better thanks to Our Dear Lady.

I.D., Illinois

FATHER WILLIAM HART MCNICHOLS
THE VIRGIN OF TENDERNESS

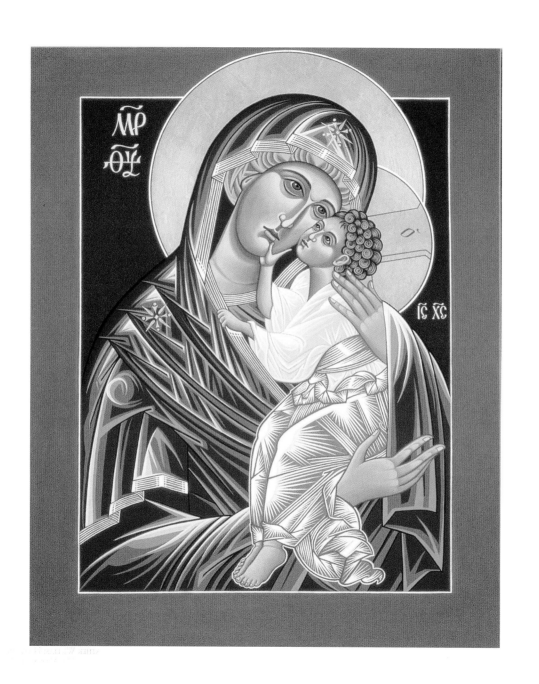

M y only daughter, Lorraine, had always been such a delightful child. Strangers often stopped to comment on her beautiful blonde hair and bright brown eyes. But more often than not, it was her constant questioning that really made people stand up and pay attention. My six boys are all very good students, but Lorraine was by far my most inquisitive.

Somewhere along the way, however, something happened. I still don't know what went wrong, but I began to really notice changes in Lorraine's behavior when she was about fifteen years old. She suddenly became quiet and reserved. She often seemed moody and edgy. And worst of all, she stopped talking and asking interesting questions. I thought it was adolescence setting in, but I was soon to learn that it was much more than that.

On October 11, 1978, my golden-haired child who I adored so much, my only daughter, Lorraine, lay in a life-threatening coma. She had overdosed on drugs.

Maybe there had been signs, signs that perhaps I had chosen to ignore all along. But all that hindsight would do me no good as I kept watch at her bedside.

For three days and three nights, Lorraine remained in a coma. And for three days and three nights, I never left her side. I cried and cried until I could cry no more. And then I began to pray. I prayed to Mary, Sweet Mother of God, who also had to endure the suffering of her child. I prayed and promised the Virgin Mother that I would do anything and everything she wanted of me, if she would just cure my beautiful golden-haired baby girl.

On the morning of the fourth day, I was awakened by a sound coming from under Lorraine's hospital bed. I knelt, looked under the bed, saw nothing, and as I rose to check on Lorraine, I saw it.

At first I thought perhaps I was dreaming, but then I realized that on the wall above Lorraine's bed was the silhouette of a woman. It was the profile of a young woman whose head was bowed as if in prayer. And then before I could blink, the profile changed to a full-figured woman with long golden hair. And as quickly as it had appeared, the image was gone. I can't even remember what I did because it all happened so fast.

But what I do remember was Lorraine's sweet voice whispering, "Mom…Mom, is that you?"

I reached for Lorraine's outstretched hand, kissed her cheek, and whispered back, "Yes, dear, it's me; it's me and Mother." And with her eyes still closed, she asked, "You mean Grammy is here too?"

"No dear, just Mother Mary."

Lorraine recovered fully, and it was not until several months later that I finally told her about the golden-haired lady in the hospital. I guess I felt like it was my secret. But to my surprise, Lorraine had kept a secret too. She told me that she had dreamed of a golden-haired lady who had told her to wake up and go to her mother.

Today Lorraine is a professional nurse with six boys of her own. She and I have kept this secret for over twenty-five years out of fear that people would think we were crazy. We recently decided that it was time to tell all. Even if we restore one person's faith in the power of prayer and the goodness of Our Lady, we will be happy.

We've both decided that we don't mind if people call us crazy. We'll take that risk.

Maria G.

28

I was getting ready to go into a meeting when the principal called me into her office. I was not afraid. Mary Gortier had always been my dear friend and confidante. But something in her voice made me nervous.

"Sarah, sit down," she said, her brows furrowed as she rubbed one hand and then the other. It was a nervous habit and one that always set my teeth on edge.

"Sarah," she said, "there has been a shooting at Columbine. Go and find your children."

And as I sped down the canyon, trying to maintain control of my nervous, twitching leg, I prayed.

"Oh, sweet Mother of God, please let me find my children and please let them be safe and unhurt. Mary, I cannot endure the loss of my children. I am not as strong as you. Please help me."

I stopped at my house just to make sure they had not come home and to check my messages for any calls. To my surprise, my son Michael, who was a sophomore at Columbine at the time, walked in the door and into my arms.

"Mom, they are shooting everyone," he sobbed. "And I couldn't find Katie. They said she was in the music room, but I looked. No one was there. Mom, I'm afraid she won't get out. We've got to go get her," he cried in anguish.

I could not believe my ears. Was this really happening to our white, suburban family in our white, suburban community? I couldn't spare another minute to think—I had to act.

"Michael, let's go," I said. "We're going to find Katie."

We headed first to the county library, which was packed with distraught parents searching for their teenagers and sobbing teenagers searching for their parents. I could not believe my eyes. And even worse, I could not believe that I too was part of this hell—this mass of lost people.

I immediately saw one of Katie's friends and begged for news. But she had not seen my Katie.

"Sarah, Sarah." I heard the voice and turned to find Debbie Riner with her arms around her daughter, Laura.

"Sarah, I just heard that some of the students are gathered over at the elementary school. I bet Katie is there," she added with hope.

I gave Debbie a hug, found Michael, and we headed out the door. But as we stepped out of the library, it was like another blow to the head. Kids and parents were running everywhere and screaming for loved ones. The elementary

32

school also was blocked off, so we decided to run through the park to the school. But we stopped short when we saw the armed soldiers and helicopters buzzing overhead.

This couldn't be happening—not on this day, not in this town.

But it was happening. And I was determined to find Katie.

I continued to pray the same prayer over and over again: "Oh, Mary, Blessed Mother, help me find my baby. Help me to find my dear sweet Katie. She has to be alright or else I will not survive."

And I prayed as I had never prayed before. "Hail Mary, Full of Grace…" And as soon as I finished the prayer, I started again.

I opened the heavy black doors to the elementary school and walked inside.

The first person I saw was Joe Anderson, the music teacher. I had known Joe for years, so I was not surprised when he grabbed my arm and looked me straight in the eyes.

"Katie got out, Sarah. Katie got out. I don't know where she is, but she's O.K. I'm sure of it," he stammered and rubbed his forehead.

But somehow I didn't believe him, and I wouldn't

believe him until I had Katie in my arms.

"But Joe, I can't find her and no one has seen her. I just don't know what to do," I wailed, all sense of hope now gone.

And then I heard it… the most wonderful word in the history of the world—delivered by the most wonderful voice.

"Mom! Mom! Mom, I'm over here!"

And it was truly music to my ears, because I could recognize that sweet, innocent voice anywhere.

And then, as I stretched my neck over the crowd, there she was—standing in the corner with tears streaming down her face—all five feet, two inches of her.

"Thank God you're alive. Thank God," I screamed and threw my arms around her.

Michael threw his big, hulky arms around us both and through his sobs I heard him whisper.

"Thank you Mary, Blessed Mother of God. Thank you for keeping us all alive."

Sarah K.

t had been a frustratingly long day. The trip to see my sister and her family was supposed to take less than two hours. And now, nine hours later, my children and I were boarding the plane that would take us to Mobile, Alabama. The Houston airport had finally reopened.

As I slowly walked to my seat, I looked out of the tiny commuter plane's window and saw that the clouds were thick with moisture, ready to open up at any moment. I saw lightning flash in the far distance and shivered as I stopped short in front of 13A.

"Ha, cruel joke," I thought. "Thirteen, unlucky, that's all."

"Unlucky, that's all." That is what my father had said both times. That's what he said when my mother had a fatal heart attack on Christmas day when I was eighteen years old. And that's what he said ten years later when he found out that he had terminal lung cancer.

I guess since then, I have been turning that phrase over and over in my brain, whenever something unpleasant happens. It has always been about luck since then. It has always been about luck or lack of it—not faith. No, faith has never been an issue with me since I had lost the two dearest people before I even reached the ripe old age of thirty.

I made certain that my children were buckled tightly and wiped the sweat from my hands as I slid into 13A. Could it be that I was going to die in a lightning storm on my twin girls' twelfth birthday? This was supposed to be their big birthday present—a surprise trip to see the aunts, uncles, and cousins that they had not seen in four years—a long time in the lives of twelve year olds. I glanced over at my fourteen-year-old son, who nodded to the sounds of Linkin Park or P.O.D. or whatever group hypnotized him at the moment. Oblivion. He is such a bright kid, I thought. How could he not see or feel the impending doom?

The pilot revved the engines; I tensed. The flight attendant demonstrated the safety precautions; I trembled. The captain cleared his throat; I swallowed hard.

"Folks, as you all know, we have had some severe weather in the Houston area today. It looks like we have been cleared for takeoff, but I would like all of you to buckle up tight. I don't like to say this and I don't say it often, but this will not be a smooth flight. The weather center has informed me that there will be lots of turbulence, but we will do the best we can to get you to Mobile, swiftly and safely."

I looked at my girls, reading quietly. *Harry Potter. The*

Princess Diaries. Innocence. They have no idea. I used to be like that—no fear. And now if you looked up fear in the dictionary, you were sure to find a picture of me.

I clenched my teeth, leaned my head back against the hard seat, and did something I had not done in years. I prayed.

"Dear Mother of God," I prayed. "I have been avoiding you since I lost my parents more than twenty years ago. But I need you now, if you really exist. I need you to save my children. I want them to have long, happy lives. Please, Mary, if you are real, if there is another world, if my parents are still alive somewhere, please let our flight be smooth today."

The really strange thing was that as soon as I finished my prayer, I unclenched my teeth and closed my eyes. I felt a wave of relaxation.

Forever the skeptic, and although I physically felt calm, I was still on guard. I felt the airplane creep down the runway, and I waited for the full engine throttle. The takeoff was flawless and before I knew it we were above the clouds—clear sky and all. I looked down at the gray and white puffy clouds and felt truly like I was floating on air, carried along by a force much greater than myself.

I must have dozed because before I knew it, the captain was again clearing his throat.

"O.K., folks, well I guess I must have lied to you. I fully expected severe turbulence, but for some strange reason, we seemed to have avoided the bumps. Well, lucky for you. Have a great day, and thanks for flying the friendly skies."

Lucky for me, ha. No, I thought, it isn't lucky for me. In fact, it's not luck at all. And for once I honestly knew that it was much, much more than luck.

Annette H.

M y mother has had hemorrhaging in her eye due to macular degeneration, for which there is no help, we were told. We started putting Lourdes water in her eyes about a month ago. When she visited the eye doctor this week, he mentioned that she had made a big improvement and she is now a candidate for treatment. We continue to use prayer and Lourdes water each day.

D.D., New York

y wife and I visited the Mother Cabrini Shrine in Denver on two occasions—first in October of 1992 and then again in May of 1993. Besides our enjoyment of the beauty of Colorado, our first trip was rather uneventful. Our second trip, however, was a life-altering experience for me.

We attended mass at St. Thomas More Catholic Church and then proceeded to the shrine. As we arrived, I remember distinctly the sweet aroma of flowers as we began the long hike up the mountain. When I mentioned it to my wife, however, her response was that I was being silly. "Of course the wildflowers are beautiful," I remember her saying, "but they don't really have an aroma." I was too engrossed with the beauty and peace of the moment to argue, so we continued on our way.

As we reached the shrine, we noticed that a huge crowd was gathering for a rosary. We immediately joined the group and as we prayed the rosary, again I experienced the sweet aroma. And again, my wife did not.

The scent became stronger and stronger until I thought I might faint. My wife commented that I looked pale and suggested that I sit. As we moved to the back of the crowd and found a place to sit, I suddenly was overcome with

Mystical Rose

emotion. I began to sweat profusely and began to feel palpitations in my chest. My wife of course wanted to take me straight to the hospital, but I refused. Then I started to cry. And when my crying turned to sobbing, I saw the fear in my wife's face.

Before I knew it, a small group had gathered around to try to help my wife, who by now was hysterical, and to also help me, who could not stop wailing. I remember one man suggesting that we call an ambulance, and my wife explaining that I did have a heart condition. But before he could even reach for his phone, and as suddenly as it had started, I stopped sobbing and the scent disappeared.

For days I could not explain what had happened to me. In fact, it was not until I returned home and saw my doctor that I realized the truth.

On June 5, 1993, I went to see Dr. Herbert, my cardiologist who had been treating me for Wolf Parkinson White Syndrome for thirty years. I told him about my experience in Denver—the shrine, the rosary, the strong scent of flowers, the sobbing—and admitted that I thought my disease was worsening. He listened attentively to my story and then remained silent for some time. His face was drawn and serious and that was when I knew it was bad news.

41

"Leo," he said with a peaceful calm. "I am not a terribly religious man, but what you have experienced can be nothing more than a miracle. Your Wolf Parkinson White Syndrome is gone and your body shows no signs that you ever had it in the first place."

My first reaction was shock of course. But as I thought about it, the whole experience now made sense. The flower scent must have been the roses that are so often associated with Our Blessed Mother, Mary. How could I have been so ignorant? It had indeed been a miracle.

That was over ten years ago, and the disease that plagued my life for three decades has not returned. I call it my "Miracle of the Roses," and I never miss a chance to share my story of how Mary, Sweet Mother of God, healed me on that beautiful May day at the Mother Cabrini Shrine in Denver, Colorado.

Leo K.

t was June 27, 2004, and I was just getting ready to go to our community pool with my three small children when I got the call. Between my children's excited yelling and my brother-in-law's muffled voice, I could barely make out three words—"Barbara… car… church." And then I heard the last and most awful word in the English language—"missing."

"Mike, hold on a second," I stammered as I turned on the children.

"Guys, please, I can't hear Uncle Mike," I pleaded.

"Quiet down! And go and wait for me outside. Now!"

I'll never forget their hurt little faces as I turned back to Mike Makowski, husband of my dear sister, Barbara.

"Paulette," he moaned. "I don't know what to do. Barbara left for church at 7:45 this morning and has not returned."

I glanced at the clock. Four twenty-five. Yikes, I thought.

"I would have called earlier, but I didn't want to alarm you. I can't reach her on her cell phone and no one has seen her."

"I called Sally Parker, who usually attends 8:15 mass as

well. She said that Barbara was not in her regular seat on the left side of the altar."

"Mike," I interrupted. "Mike, you've got to call the police."

"I did, Paulette, and they said that she's not a missing person until after twenty-four hours."

My stomach ached and I felt sweat forming on my forehead.

"Then you'll have to find her yourself," I snapped, well aware of my callousness.

It seemed like hours before Mike called a second time.

"Paulette," he whispered. "Sit down. And sit down now."

I felt my body tense and my breath stop.

"Paulette, Barbara has had an accident, but she's alive," he said. And then he began to tell me the story—the story that would change my life forever.

On Sunday, June 27, 2004, my sister, Barbara Stephens Makowski was on her way to 8:15 mass when her car skidded off of the road. Her car hit several trees and came to a stop about seventy-five feet down into a ravine. She had been knocked unconscious and suffered a severe

44

concussion. She was airlifted to Nashville Central Hospital where she remained for several weeks—battered, bruised, but alive!

But she never would have been found if it had not been for Barbara's neighbor, whose little four-year-old boy, Patrick, made the discovery. As soon as Mike had alerted the neighborhood, Patrick had insisted that he knew where Mrs. Makowski had gone. He had insisted that his father drive him around so that he could show him the location. Patrick's father, Frank Harrington, was skeptical, but thought it was worth a try.

As Patrick instructed, Frank headed down Hwy 14. After about fifteen minutes, Patrick told his father to stop the car and said that Mrs. Makowski was "down there," referring to a deep ravine. Frank shined his flashlight down the ravine, and there it was—a tan Honda Civic on its side and against a tree.

And if that was not enough to restore my faith, the first thing that Barbara told me when she came out of intensive care was that she had had a near death experience. She told me how the Blessed Virgin Mother had appeared to her and had held her in her arms with a gentleness and peace she had never felt before. And she added that Mary's beauty was indescribable. She said that Our Lord was there too but only for an instant. And when I asked her to describe him, she could not. She said she saw him only for a second but that she would feel him forever. And I believe her.

So that is the story about what happened to my sister in June of this year—the story that has helped me to discover that we as humans know only a fraction of what there is to know about our world and our connection to the spiritual world.

Paulette L.

46

My granddaughter Katie was one year old when she developed a painful tremor on her right foot. She had difficulty walking and doctors could not diagnose the problem. While taking Katie to a neurologist, her mother rubbed her afflicted foot with water from a bottle of Lourdes water. This doctor could not find a diagnosis either but Katie never had a problem again.

A.P., Colorado

It was at what I thought was the height of my spiritual life that I realized the goodness of Mary. I had been a seamstress for the statue of Our Blessed Mother at St. Francis of Assisi for about four years when my friend encouraged me to run for the elective position of sacristan. The primary duty of the sacristan is to take care of the sacristy, the room in the church that houses the sacred vessels and vestments. In addition, I would be responsible for sewing clothing for Our Lady. Of course I did not think I was worthy, but my friend would not give up. To my amazement, I ran and I won.

47

The next five years were wonderful. I devoted many hours to my job as sacristan and loved every minute of it. At no time did I feel closer to Mary than those five years. I never had visions, but I always felt her presence. It was a quiet and peaceful presence, almost like a constant reminder that I was in good hands, like someone was always watching over me.

Then my mother got sick. She was told she had terminal cancer and would not live more than six months. I was devastated. I kicked and cried and begged God for his mercy. I asked Mary to intervene and to take care of my mother. And I waited for the cure.

But the cure didn't come. So I sewed and sewed and sewed. My mother's favorite color was lilac, so I made her a new lilac dress. I made the Blessed Mother an identical dress as an offering with hopes that perhaps she would hear my prayers and cure my mother.

But my mother got weaker. I got the call at about 2 p.m. I was needed right away at the hospital. My mother wanted me to bring the lilac dress for her. In the meantime, I called my assistant, Amanda, and told her that she would be in charge of the sacristy and of dressing the Blessed Mother.

"Choose whatever clothing you want, I trust your judgment," I told Amanda. "My mother is very ill and I don't know when I'll return." Somehow I knew that my mother's days were numbered. And somehow I couldn't help but feel betrayed. Had Mary not heard my prayers? Hadn't I been her dutiful servant for all of these years?

As I walked into her hospital room, something felt strange. Mother's face was ashen but her smile was unusually radiant. My mother had always been known for her wide smile and beautiful teeth. She had a way of brightening up a room, and today she had filled it with sunshine.

She meekly asked the nurses and doctor to leave, and she gestured for me to come closer to her bed. It was only a whisper but I knew right away.

"She came to me last night. Blessed Mother came to me last night. She told me everything was in place. She told me to wear my lilac dress. She told me it was time."

A tear rolled down her cheek as she smiled at me again, trying to assure me that it would be O.K. She took my hand and looked at me. "Mary," she said. "Please don't be sad. I am ready. And you will be too when it is your time. The secret is that she prepares us all as she has prepared me." My mother looked at me, squeezed my hand, closed her eyes, and whispered, "I love you, Mary." And then she drifted off to sleep.

The next day as I went into the church to discuss my mother's funeral mass with Father John, I was struck by an incredible sight—Amanda had dressed the Blessed Mother in her lilac dress. How could she have known? I specifically had told her to make her own choices.

I knew then that Mother Mary had not deserted me. It was only a whisper, but she had answered my prayers. She had taken care of my mother after all.

Mary D.

For as long as I can remember, I have gone with my grandmother to visit La Conquistadora. Following her into the dim abode and stone cathedral, I dip my index finger into the silver bowl of holy water and carefully cross myself. As I murmur the blessings solemnly, I make the sign of the cross. The rows of pews are empty and the air echoes as the heavy door closes behind us. Eyes on the worn red carpet, I make my way to a carved wooden pew and, like my grandmother, duck my head quickly and cross myself again as I sit down. It is cool in the church and rows of candles in their glass holders flicker in the shadows.

Beside me, my grandmother bows her head, a glittering burst of color in her bright dress and gleaming jewelry. Her perfume smells like lipstick, gold shoes and margaritas. She is in her element chatting during intermission at the opera or laughing gaily with the waiters when she goes out to lunch. Her hands, though, are devout, wrinkled, and rough, her nails clean and short. She rolls each silver prayer between her fingers, intuitively, as if the rosary has worn a track in her palms. I, too, bow my head to pray, but my thoughts stray.

I look up into the face of La Conquistadora. She is

perched high above the back altar, small and silent and poised. I marvel at the crudeness of her carved face, the simple lines of her nose and high forehead. Her filmy dress falls lightly around her small wooden body and the soft layers hide her feet. Rows of candles surround her and later when I carefully light my own prayer, my grandmother guiding my hand gently, the smell of wax and burnt matches will sting my nostrils. La Conquistadora, Our Lady of the Conquest, was brought over by the Spaniards for protection during their conquest of New Spain, and for three hundred years she has looked over the bowed heads of my family.

While my grandmother prays beside me, her soft, rapid whisper washing over me like a shiver, the power and beauty of this place is suddenly exhilarating. I lean my head back, studying the elaborate paintings on the arched ceiling of the cathedral—the swirls of angels, stars, and nameless robed men and women with outstretched hands, dimmed by two centuries of candle smoke. My stomach drops as I look up into the depths of the cathedral. Sitting in the hard pew, I feel tiny in the awesome expanse of still air and I can feel the history that surrounds me like an echo.

My family's frequent moves have left me rich in experiences, discoveries, and friendships. But I always look

51

forward to returning to Santa Fe. There I am surrounded by the redolent pinions and embraced by my family's history. Looking into La Conquistadora's face, I feel the pull of my feet in sandy arroyos and my eyes burn with the sharp smell of roasted chili. These visits with my grandmother to the Cathedral of St. Francis mark my return home.

Kirstin Q.

For more than two years my wife has had a big mole on her back that has caught the attention of several well-meaning people who encouraged her to go to the doctor. Neither of us had been too concerned because her family's makeup includes skin moles. Around Thanksgiving time she saw a dermatologist who was very alarmed and said he was sure it was cancer. We started praying and using Lourdes water right away. We asked Our Lady to intercede and ask the Lord for a healing. We prayed the cancer would not spread. She had surgery and we were blessed with the favor we had asked.

B. S., Maryland

It was the call every parent dreads. A friend phoned Cat and Richard to say they had seen their son Joe's Volvo in a wreck. Cat and Richard hurried to the scene to find their son in the crumpled car—he had been hit head-on by a drunk driver. As they waited, the rescue team arrived and Joe was quickly airlifted to the hospital in serious condition.

After reaching the hospital, Joe's parents were told he had head injuries and was in a coma. He was immediately put in ICU.

The Stones were overwhelmed by the trauma, but amazed and grateful at the outpouring of support from the community that punctuated the event. People had stopped at the accident scene and stayed. Before his parents even knew what was happening, Joe was the center of a number of prayer chains that spread from church to church. Friends kept coming to the hospital, and at one point there were so many people in the waiting room, they got in trouble with one of the nurses.

People supported the family by providing food, and even helping clean the Stone's house while the parents stayed at Joe's side.

It was on the third day of the ordeal, with Joe still in a

coma, that the mother of one of Joe's friends, Maria, brought in a small bottle of Lourdes water. Cat had already been praying and, although Lutheran, followed the woman's directions and applied the water to Joe's head, face, neck and shoulders, then left the room to allow one of Joe's friends to visit him.

Within twenty minutes, Joe's friend came bounding back down the hall saying, "He's opened his eyes, he's awake, he's awake."

Cat raced down the hall to find her son lying in bed with his eyes open for the first time since the accident.

Wanting to share the news with the world, Cat tried to remember the phone number for Joe's coach—a man Joe was very close to and one who could get the word out. While fumbling to find the coach's number, Cat was stunned when Joe himself carefully recited the coach's number.

Since then, Joe's improvement has been strong and steady. And the prognosis—he'll be just fine.

Cat S.

FATHER WILLIAM HART MCNICHOLS
MOTHER OF GOD, QUEEN OF PILGRIMS

55

My sister organized a reunion for our huge family last August. For anyone else, it would have been no big deal. But you see, my sister was on her deathbed in July.

My sister has had a rare lung disease that has plagued her for several years. Twice she had been near death and twice she had called in the lawyers to sign the "Do not resuscitate" papers. Last July, Dr. Stanley told us that any disease of the lungs was incredibly difficult to cure, and that her case was hopeless. I could tell it was almost as difficult for him to tell us as it was for us to hear that my sister would not be with us much longer.

But I was not so willing to let go. After all, my sister had always been like a mother to me. Eight years older and eighty years wiser, my sister had been the one who took control and pulled our family together after our parents died. I realized, as Dr. Stanley patted my shoulder and pursed his lips, that it was my turn to step up to the plate.

Father Michael W. was a dear friend of mine and would know what to do. As I reached for the big brass handle of the church door, I was surprised to see it open by itself.

"Father Michael," I gasped. "I was just going to look for you."

56

"How wonderful to be needed," he smiled that warm, Father Michael smile.

"What can I do for you, dear?" he asked.

"It's Margie…" I gulped. The words wouldn't form as I thought of Dr. Stanley and his prognosis of doom.

"Barb, follow me," said Father Michael, and he motioned me to the vestibule at the back of the church.

Father Michael reached behind the statue of the Blessed Mother and pulled out a small golden box with a beautiful lace bow tied around its tiny perimeter.

"This is what I call a 'miraculous medal of Mary," he said and made the sign of the cross over the tiny box.

"Give it to your sister, tell her to wear it every day, morning and night, and all of you pray for God's blessing and Mary's miracles."

"Now go, and let dear Margie be healed." And again, Father Michael made the sign of the cross—this time on my forehead.

Of course I did everything that Father Michael told me to do—and so did Margie.

That was July 7, 2002. By July 25, my sister, Margie Hanson Benoir, was a new and totally cured woman without an ounce of illness in her lungs. On August 27, our family celebrated the first annual Hanson reunion, which Margie organized in less than a month—"The Hanson Reunion of Hope," I like to call it, because it reminded us all that if we believe and trust in the goodness of Our Lord and Blessed Mother, there is always hope.

Barb T.

In March of 2002 I was diagnosed with breast cancer. I had lots of support from family, friends, and doctors. However, the real breakthrough came for me when a dear friend gave me a bottle of Lourdes water. I had just been told that my first surgery was unsuccessful and that I would require a second. I sat at my bedside and cried and prayed like I had never prayed before. I drank the water and bowed my head. I felt a strong sense of peace. When I spoke to my surgeon after the second surgery, she said that they had found no remaining cancer cells and that I was all clear. No one will ever convince me that I didn't experience my own miracle that night through the holy Mother's intercession.

N.O., Illinois

59

sk any woman whose mother has died and I guarantee she will tell you that she is forever changed, that she is forever at a loss, that she is forever empty. My mother died when I was a mere babe—a month and a half to be exact. No, I never knew my mother, but I always knew her absence affected me for all of my life—as a child, as a teenager, and as an adult.

As a child, I was a loner. I was insecure and withdrawn, so it is no surprise that in eighth grade, I decided my life was worthless. My father had recently remarried and I felt like I had been replaced. Looking back, I suppose those feelings were normal, but at the time, I felt isolated and unloved. That is when I met Jackie. Jackie was a bad influence to say the least. She got me into smoking, drinking, and drugs. I started lying and we started living in another world in order to find some type of escape from our loneliness.

Well, one thing led to another and before I knew it I was twenty-two, married, and pregnant. My husband and I were heavy into drugs at the time. I didn't know what I was doing, so when he insisted that I have an abortion, I listened to him. I was lost and being carried along by this man who had said he loved me. Two years passed and I found myself

60

pregnant again. Jim did not want me to have the child, but this time I insisted on keeping it. He left me, nevertheless, but somehow I found the strength to raise our daughter alone. I was determined that my daughter would have a mother, unlike me.

Six months later, though, I found myself living in a trailer park with my sister and my baby girl. I was depressed, lonely, broke, and utterly dejected. I contemplated suicide. I phoned my friend who told me she would be right over. I told her it would be too late. But it wasn't too late, because as I took the razor blade and looked into the mirror, I heard a voice. I mean, I really heard a voice, an audible voice and not just one in my head. The voice said, "God doesn't make junk." I dropped the razor, ran to my daughter, and sobbed. How could I even think of leaving my little girl motherless? I promised that I would never again be such a fool.

After that my life began to change. I found a job, started dating nice men, and even started going to church. I met a friend at church who started talking to me about a place called Medjugorje. I was somewhat skeptical, but listened anyway about the miracles and visions of Mary. After several months, Teri convinced me to go with her. I had a little money saved up but not nearly enough. But before I could even tell Teri that I wouldn't be able to afford it, an odd thing happened. A radio station called me out of the blue and after answering a simple question about the Blues Brothers, a band I knew lots about, they informed me that I had won $500. I was shocked. Then a friend called to ask if I wanted to make some extra money babysitting for her son while she was out of town on business for two weeks. Before I knew it, I had the money and was on a plane to Medjugorje with Teri.

In the five years following my trip to Medjugorje, I have experienced visions of Mary and have received messages from the Lord. What I would like to tell you about now, though, is what I consider my first experience with Our Blessed Mother.

On the first night in Medjugorje, I couldn't sleep so I went outside on the porch to pray. One of the men from our group, John, was walking by and asked if I wanted to walk up Apparition Hill with him. As we began to ascend the hill, we saw a small dark figure sitting on a rock. As we approached the figure, we discovered it was a little old woman from the village. She stopped us and proceeded to tell us the story of Medjugorje from a villager's point of view. The astounding thing was that she was speaking Croatian. I realized partway through the story that I understood everything she was saying, and so I started translating to John. He asked how I knew what she was saying. I responded that I didn't know. Then about halfway through the conversation, I stopped understanding her and John, to his amazement, started interpreting to me. We were both in shock and kept exchanging glances of astonishment. She then motioned for us to follow her up the hill.

Sure, follow an eighty-five-year-old woman up a steep hill, I thought. There's no way she will make it. Well, she took us by the hand, and this little old woman started racing up the hill like a long distance runner. We could hardly keep up with her. When we reached the summit, she took us to every cross, stopping to pray and walking circles around us as she did so. John and I exchanged no words, but we could both feel the wonder and awe at what was taking place. God's presence was strong, and we both knew it. After we finished the last cross, we started walking down the hill in silence. We both knew that something had just happened, but we weren't quite sure what it was, other than wonderful prayer. At the bottom of the hill, the woman came to a sudden stop and turned to look at us. We introduced ourselves and then asked her name. She looked up at the sky and then to us. John and I both knew then that this was no ordinary woman. When she turned from the sky to us, she looked fifty years younger. She then very quietly, almost in a whisper, said, "My name is Gospa."

"Oh," John responded, surprising me and I think, himself, "You mean, like the Blessed Mother, Mary."

She said, "Gospa, yes, Mary in Croatian."

We looked at each other and turned back to look at her, but she was gone. I mean, GONE!

We headed back to our rooms in silence. When I arrived in my room, my friend Teri was frantic.

"Where have you been?" she screamed. "We're in this Communist country, you take off all night, and you expect me to be calm?"

Before I could speak, Marie, a woman who was rooming with us, said calmly, "She's been with the Mother of God."

I just looked at her in shock. "I suppose that's where I've been," I realized. "Yes," I said. "That's exactly where I've been."

To say the least that was a turning point in my life. And since then, I have never again felt that sorrow and longing and emptiness that comes with living without a mother. For, you see, I realized that night that I do indeed have a mother—Mary, Mother of God, and I suppose, of me.

Veronica G.

It was a Sunday afternoon in Santa Fe and the first year that the tradition of La Conquistadora's May procession was finally being restored. The Caballeros carried La Conquistadora on a bier from the school with some three hundred faithful singing Marian songs in procession. As she was placed in the sanctuary, before the rosary, there was a small commotion as a crack at the base was discovered after the ceremony took place.

It was Pedro who noticed it first.

"Mark," he said to me, "it's a crack…in the base…Our Lady, she falls apart," He pointed out the large separation between the statue and the base.

"Mark, can she be repaired?" he asked, with sad eyes.

Since that unusually hot and humid day in Santa Fe last May, I have been restoring La Conquistadora. And while this might seem like the restoration of a holy icon, to those who do not know, La Conquistadora is much more than a statue. She is, in fact, a very important symbol to the people of Santa Fe because she represents Santa Fe's faith and devotion.

The Battle of Santa Fe, a bloody, two-day siege, occurred in 1662 when rebels attempted to take back the settlement that was originally overrun by Native American insurgents. La Conquistadora was hastily carried from Santa Fe to El Paso by a young mother, who rescued her from certain destruction. She was the only symbol of the people's faith that survived the uprising. The legend goes that as men carried her into battle, they prayed for victory. When it came, they promised to honor her each year with a fiesta, procession, and novena.

I was asked to examine her status after the crack was discovered. I knew that La Conquistadora had an interesting history, and I wanted to make sure that our preservation was first rate. She had been modified and restored many times in the past with the last preservation performed by the artist Bauman in the 1930s. A base was added in the late 1940s with old altar decorations to commemorate the destruction of the atom bombs. In fact, La Conquistadora traveled to White Sands, New Mexico, where the first nuclear test blast occurred.

After her theft and attempted ransoming by youths in the early 1970s, her damaged face was touched up. Interestingly, the story goes that the safest place to keep her the night of her recovery was the local jail where Pedro, a devoted servant, spent the night "locked up" with her.

CHERI LOMONTE
MARY WITH TURQUOISE CROWN

When Pedro and I disassembled the base of the statue, the first step in her preservation, we discovered that she was hollow. I found a sealed door in her back and continued to examine the interior with a flexible probing mirror. Pedro suggested that we have her x-rayed, so he immediately called St. Vincent's Hospital and made the arrangement.

The x-ray showed a pole with a decorative ball on top in her inner cavity. A small piece of white, hand-woven cloth was also found in this "secret" inner chamber. After a trip to the library, later that week, I found evidence that these items were part of a banner that soldiers typically carried into battle. Thus, it seemed that the legend might be true— she was indeed carried into battle to reclaim Santa Fe.

As Pedro and I continued our work, I realized that the labor itself was a form of prayer for me. I always prayed before and during our preservation of La Conquistadora. Sometimes, as I entered the brightly sunlit room in the back of the cathedral where we worked, it seemed that her facial expression would change. It wasn't an eerie feeling at all; in fact, it was rewarding to think that perhaps La Conquistadora was pleased with our toils.

My experience those several months made me rekindle my relationship with the Blessed Mother, and made me realize as well that she is the mother of us all. Her intercession in our lives is invaluable and absolutely necessary for a healthy, happy, and balanced life, for all of her actions and all of our prayers are aimed at Christ, our true savior. My experience also made me realize that her role has not changed over the past thousands of years. In fact, it is perhaps more vital today than ever in history.

Mark H.

My husband Tom was scheduled for lung surgery because medical methods to relieve his condition were not working. I applied Lourdes water to his chest and said prayers many times during the day. With Mary's intervention, and a medicine they injected in him that they did not have high hopes of working, he got better. Surgery was cancelled. Thank you, Blessed Mother.

V.S., Florida

My heritage is Native American and as a Native American I have always been taught to revere my elders. In particular, my culture teaches a special reverence for mothers who are the true givers of life. My grandmother used to say, "Mothers will hold our hands at both ends of life."

I have always loved that saying and I have always loved my grandmother for instilling in me a love for the Blessed Mother. She taught me to respect Mary and to pray to her in times of need.

When I went off to Vietnam back in the 1960s, my grandmother gave me a medal of the Virgin Mary and told me to wear it always, for it would keep me out of harm's way. But after a month in Vietnam and, in fact, during the first real battle that I was in, I lost the medal. And needless to say, I was devastated. I prayed and prayed to the Virgin Mary that I would find it.

Time passed, but I never forgot about my medal and I never found it either. One day though, a priest arrived and joined our company. He was a kind man, and one with whom I felt comfortable talking to about my faith.

On one particular Sunday, Father Greene told me that

he wanted to say Easter mass for the troops but didn't have a cross for the service. I told him not to worry; I would make one for him.

I have no idea how, but I managed to make quite an elaborate six-foot cross for him in a matter of days. In fact, as I was finishing the cross, I began to tell him about the medal that I had lost during the first month in Vietnam. I actually thought it was rather odd that he didn't really show any empathy—no words of kindness or concern—but instead excused himself and said he'd be back soon.

Well, he did come back and quickly, I might add. And again he had no words. This time though he held out his fist to me, turned it over and opened it. And to my surprise, there it was—my medal. I just looked at him in awe, and this time I had no words.

"On my first day here, I said a mass in the field and as I was giving the Eucharist, a shiny object on the ground caught my eye," he said. "When I realized it was a medal, I picked it up, put it in my pocket, and forgot about it until you told me your story. You see, I truly believe that when you give, you always get back, three-fold."

"You are so right, Father Greene," I smiled. "And this is truly a miracle."

I absolutely knew that finding that medal was a miracle. And I knew that the Blessed Mother had been with me the whole time. And I knew too that she had been holding me in her arms as I worked as a "tunnel rat" during those months of absolute fear and terror in Vietnam.

Lench A.

It just so happens my dog's name is "Echo," a thirteen-year-old black Labrador retriever. In October 2001, my dog was falling down, vomiting and urinating blood. I knew it was a very serious condition and took Echo to two separate veterinarian clinics to confirm my worst fears: brain cancer. Three different doctors all shared the same opinion—my dog had seven to ten days to live. She had stopped eating completely for six days. I started a regular routine of putting Lourdes water in the cup of my hand so she could drink out of it every night. I am happy to say that we are celebrating well over a year since Echo was diagnosed. Truly a miracle.

D.S., Connecticut

73

Our Lady came to me on a rainy June morning in 1986 after the 7:00 a.m. mass at Our Lady of Fatima Catholic Church. I had just lit a candle to the Virgin Mary and had returned to my pew to kneel and pray for my mother who had recently died, when I saw the light from the candle.

It flickered and then became very bright, almost blinding me so that I had to turn my head and blink. I thought I was imagining it when a figure of a lady came toward me. She was probably about three feet away from me, and my first instinct was to back up. And as I backed away, the figure turned from Our Lady of Fatima into La Conquistadora and then again into Our Lady of Guadalupe. The lady spoke, but her lips did not move. She told me not to be afraid and specifically said, "Here I am, this is who I am."

But I guess I didn't listen because I stood up, fell backwards, and ran out of the church. I was petrified.

When I walked in the door of my home, I remember that the first words to come from my husband's mouth were, "Your eyes, Vangi, they're shining. What's happened to you?" I thought it was odd that my husband, who isn't a very religious person, immediately believed me when I told him of the vision. "You have to go back," he said. "She's trying to tell you something."

Of course I knew he was right. And although I was terrified, I did go back to church the next day. By then I had convinced myself that it was all my imagination, that I had been overtired, that I would see nothing.

But I was wrong. Immediately as I knelt in front of the altar, I felt a strange sensation, like a warm chill running through my body. I looked up and saw that this time the statue of Our Lady was glowing in a bluish light. And again, she spoke but her lips did not move. She said, "Here I am, this is who I am." This time I did not run, but instead I continued to kneel as the vision slowly faded.

The third day, I returned again to church and this time, I saw nothing. But as I knelt, I heard a whisper: "Here I am, this is who I am." I must have stared at the statue for an hour before I realized that the message was clear. I closed my eyes and said aloud, "I know it's you." And then, as I opened my eyes, I saw her. She was the most beautiful woman I had ever seen. Her lips were a soft pink and her eyes seemed clear, with a slight tinge of blue around the edges. And again she spoke, but her lips did not move. She said, "Fast, cleanse your body, gain strength, and don't worry." And then, "I need your help. Gather your family, have a meal together, and pray."

I knew then that my task was great. I had to tell my five brothers and five sisters that I was seeing visions of Mary. Well, I must tell you that my mother raised us in a strict, religious environment, but as we grew up, not all of us have continued our faith. I knew that my youngest brother, Gerald, would think that I had lost my mind. But I also knew that I had to deliver the message and gather my family. I did manage to get everyone to come to my house a few days later. We were all still living in the same area, so it made it a little easier to get them together. I still think it was amazing, though, that all of them could make it on that Thursday night, since we all did have jobs and different schedules. Anyway, as we gathered that evening, I'll never forget the heavy silence as I told them. And then Gerald's eyes glazed over and he spoke: "Here I am, this is who I am."

I gasped and fell into my mother's antique rocker. I had not told him the specifics, yet. How could he know?

"Gerald, what did you say?" I asked.

"I didn't say a word," he said and looked at me as if I had just asked him to recite the Periodic Table. I looked at my other siblings as they nodded and repeated his words. There

was no denying it, everyone had heard.

That was really the beginning of the messages. Our Lady continued to speak through Gerald as we met every Thursday evening after that. She told us to prepare, to pray, to fast and, most of all, to keep the messages in the family, for now.

That was June. In September, she appeared to us and told us that it was time. And that is when we started to tell our friends and neighbors what was happening. We invited them to say the rosary with us. Then, before we knew it, strangers were coming to our house. Everyone wanted to know the truth. Everyone wanted to see her too. And although we knew it was real, not everyone believed us. In fact, many people thought we were fools and needed to be committed.

And we understood the skeptics. Of course, it seemed absurd that Mary, Mother of God would be speaking to our family. But we continued to invite strangers into our home, and we continued to feed them and nourish them as Mary had instructed us.

And although no one else actually experienced the visions, Mary continued to speak to our family, through Gerald and sometimes through me.

One October evening as we gathered for our weekly rosary, we received a different sort of message. Usually our messages were general, but this one in particular was very specific. Our Lady instructed us to go to the Cross of the Martyrs, which was on top of a small hill in our town. She told us to gather our followers and there she would give them a sign.

We had at least two hundred people that evening as we gathered at the base of the hill. The night sky was glowing, and I remember looking around at all the expectant faces, as they too seemed to notice the brilliant blue sky.

But when we were about halfway up the hill, out of nowhere came the crash of thunder and rain—lots and lots of rain. The priest who was leading us yelled to all, "Go back!" But oddly, no one listened. Instead, the crowd started to sing and pray in unison and continued to climb the steep hill in the rain and thunder.

When we reached the top of the hill the storm intensified. Everyone by this time was soaking wet and blinded by the driving rain.

And then we heard it. Pounding. It was soft at first, but then the pounding became so loud that we had to cover our ears. Gerald began to speak to the crowd and I thought how amazing it was that we could hear his words with all of the pounding.

But we all heard his words very clearly: "I am purifying everyone, trust me and hear the passion of the Lord." He paused and then continued, "Fasting, praying, adoration, sacraments, simplicity, love, unity. These must be your goals for salvation. I have come to bring you back to my Son. Now go back and spread the word."

But this was not the only miracle that we would experience that day. When we arrived at the bottom of the hill, the rain suddenly stopped, and we looked in awe at each other as we noticed that our clothes were completely dry.

After that day, we no longer saw or heard Our Lady, but my family as well as many others have been changed forever because of our experience. We talk about how loving and giving and compassionate we have all become as a result. Our lives now seem to have meaning like never before.

And while I know that there will always be skeptics, I also know that there will always be the faithful as well. As for me, I like to consider myself among the faithful because I know in my heart that everything that I experienced in those five months in 1986 was true and real and really and truly divine.

Vangi P.

80

had thirteen fractures, a broken jaw, a broken wrist, a smashed ankle, and seven crushed vertebrae. And I was the lucky one. Although I don't really think it was luck. I firmly believe that the Blessed Mother saved my roommate, Denise, and me on that fateful night in November of 1969. I don't remember much, but I do remember reaching in the back seat of the car and getting my miraculous medal. I don't know how I did it with all of my broken bones, but I know that I held onto that medal as I was wheeled into the emergency room at Seattle's Providence Hospital. And I remember praying to the Blessed Mother to save my friend Denise and me.

I also remember a nurse coming into my room a few days later and handing me my medal.

"I found this in the emergency room and one of the nurses said that she saw it in your hand when you arrived here on Sunday." She smiled as she placed the miraculous medal in my hand.

I held it in there and prayed and thanked Mary for sparing my life. And I promised that I would do whatever I could to serve and spread the message about the medal.

That was many years ago. Denise and I still talk about

how truly blessed we are to have survived such a horrific accident, even after being given the last rites. Denise never really talks about her years of therapy, and I know that she has learned to accept the fact that one of her legs had to be amputated. She is an amazing person and friend, and Denise too has dedicated her life to spreading the word and the goodness of Mary, the Blessed Mother.

Caroline F.

82

Recently I was to have surgery on my leg to open a blocked artery. I started to use my Lourdes water. My surgery was supposed to have been in April. I was ready for surgery, however, the doctor examined my leg again and said, "You can go home, and you do not need surgery—the blockage is opened." I had been taking medication to open the artery, but it had not helped. I know the Lourdes water did.

F.N., New York

ourteen years ago I was diagnosed with cancer. My children were in first and third grade, and I remember thinking that I could not leave them motherless in a difficult world.

On the day that my doctor gave me the horrid diagnosis, I went home and fell to my knees and prayed. And I asked the Blessed Mother for divine intervention. In particular, I asked her to spare me and to keep me alive until my children graduated from high school.

I had always been an optimistic person, but several weeks later, when my doctor told me that my cancer looked worse than he had originally thought, I was devastated. My whole reality changed with his words: "mastectomy" and "chemotherapy."

For several weeks, I walked around in a fog. How could this be happening in my happy world?

On Monday, October 23, three weeks from the day that I had received my death sentence, I found the strength to tell my children. I assured them that everything would be fine, but that I would need their help and patience for the next several months.

Michael, my youngest, said nothing. He looked at me with his big blue eyes and eyelashes as long as the Mississippi River, and then ran up to his room. I knew that it would take him awhile, and so I left him alone to try to understand as best a bright, first grader could.

Katie, my third grader, threw her arms around my neck and sobbed. "Mommy, I don't want you to die," she cried. And joining in her outpouring, I felt the tears stream down my cheek.

"Katie," I whispered. "All you have to do is to pray to Mary, Mother of Jesus. Pray that I will be strong and will beat this ugly disease," I told her.

And as if she had been silenced from above, Laura stopped her crying.

"Yes, Mommy," she said as she wiped the tears from her red and puffy eyes.

"Mary will save you if you and I believe, right, Mommy"?

I stroked her silky blonde hair and held her close. "Katie, you are absolutely right," I said, smiling.

Today, I have lived to see both of my children walk down the aisle and receive their diplomas—not only from high school but from college as well.

Some people say that I was one of the lucky ones, but I know that it wasn't luck that cured my cancer. It was Mary, the Blessed Mother of God who answered my prayers and those of my dear sweet Katie.

Sarah K.

Help me with all my heart and soul for I love you with all my heart and soul.

When my son came back from Vietnam with a life-threatening virus he was a mere eighteen years old. I remember how we all were so happy that he was home yet sad that he was so ill. I couldn't believe that my precious blonde, blue-eyed boy might not see his nineteenth birthday.

At the time, I was very active in my church. In fact, I was responsible for making, washing, ironing, and caring for the purificators, the white sheets on the altar that hold the host and wine. I had been performing this duty for about fifteen years when Martin returned from Vietnam a broken man.

I remember one particular Saturday morning, as I was placing the purificator on the altar I had this feeling that I should kneel and pray to La Conquistadora. My knees were going bad, but I knelt anyway. I asked the Holy Mother of God, with all my heart and soul, to help me. "I love you with all my heart and soul, Mary. You know how it is to lose a son. Oh, please, have mercy and save my boy. Make him whole again and cure his virus."

I returned home that morning to a call from my daughter, Suzi. "Martin is really sick, Mom. He is on his way to the hospital for more testing," she said nervously. "He wants you to meet him there, Mom. I tried to go with him, but he wouldn't hear of it," Suzi muttered.

I rushed to the hospital and the first thing Dr. Michaels told me was that Martin would not make it. I heard his words, but they did not register. And I think I even surprised myself when I looked him straight in the eye and said, "Dr. Michaels, you are wrong. Martin will make it and the Blessed Virgin Mother will make sure of that."

The next day, Martin was notified that he was at the top of the list for a liver transplant. The next few months were crucial, but I never worried a bit. I truly knew that Mary would heal my son.

And that she did. Yes, Martin did see his nineteenth birthday. In fact, he is fifty-one years old with grown children of his own. He not only survived the virus, but after his recovery, he thrived in every aspect of his life. Today most people call him Dr. Martin Diego, and he now helps to heal others.

Everyday, I thank the Virgin Mary and never forget to say, "I love you with all my heart and soul."

Miquela S.

I t's time," Sister Margarite smiled, her green eyes gleaming as she handed me the powdery blue gown. My heart pounded inside my chest. I hesitated at the water's edge, and felt the cold of the October air. Pneumonia, I thought, the doctors told me not to get cold or that would be the end of me. I shivered as I looked at my reflection in the clear, calm water.

Could this be real? Had I, the woman who had been given the Last Rites, seven times, really traveled all the way to Lourdes in Southern France, despite my condition and my doctors' orders? Had I really defied even my own dear husband? Poor Carlos, what would he do with his crazy wife?

"Just step in slowly, Mercedes," Sister Margarite said, nodding as her soft, warm hand held mine. My toe hit the water—ice cold. A million thoughts raced through my brain: I'm going to die—I'll get even sicker—I won't live to see my grandchildren—poor Carlos. Ha, I thought, my nickname, "A Woman of Faith," sure doesn't seem to fit me now.

"It's O.K., both feet now." Sister Margarite held my hand tightly and smiled, this time her beautiful white teeth seemed to glow in the evening light. I closed my eyes, took a deep breath, sank low in the frigid water, and prayed to the Virgin Mary to heal my sick heart: "Mary, Mother of God, I don't know why I was born with a defective heart; I don't know why my heart is bleeding into my lungs; I don't know why the surgeries have not worked. But Mary, I do know that I believe in you and your powerful grace. If it is your will, please mend my bad heart."

"Now step out slowly, Mercedes." Sister Margarite looked like an angel in her pure white robe as she beckoned me towards the robe. "Here, put this on, dear," she said, and made the sign of the cross on my forehead. I remember the strange feeling as I put on the robe, like something was different inside of me...like something was perhaps...normal?

That was 1958 and the doctors are probably still wondering how I came home from Lourdes that October with a new heart, a "normal" heart as Dr. McLean called it. But I am not wondering and have never wondered...I have always known that Our Blessed Mother cured me and allowed me to live a long and happy life.

Mercedes T.

believe in miracles.

Last April, my forty-year-old niece was diagnosed with malignant melanoma. At the time, she had a fourteen-year-old son and a two-year-old daughter. To say that the family was shocked and horrified would be an understatement.

Rena's prognosis was good at first, but after several rounds of chemotherapy, the doctors called the family together and admitted that her body was not responding to the treatment. They would have to change the treatment and give stronger and more frequent chemotherapy.

The following months were difficult as Rena was always exhausted and frustrated by the loss of her control. She was always a very organized person who kept her family on track. And she was beginning to realize that things would never be the same.

One day when I was visiting with her, Rena admitted that she could lose her battle with cancer. She sobbed in my arms; we both sobbed actually, and then I had an epiphany. I remembered my sister-in-law, her miraculous recovery from lung disease…and Father Michael.

After leaving Rena's house, I headed over to the church.

"I suppose it is selfish to ask for two miracles from one family, but Father Michael, I need your help," I said as I wiped away a tear.

"We live in a small town," said Father Michael. "I am well aware of Rena's illness. I have been praying for her, and I half expected your visit, in fact."

"I know that your sister-in-law, Margie Hanson, has made a full recovery from lung disease. And I also know that God works in mysterious ways," he said as he handed me the medal.

"Go in peace and pray to Mary, the Mother of God, like you have never prayed before."

I left the church that Thursday morning with the medal in my hand and hope in my heart, and I went straight to Rena's house to place the medal around her neck.

On Tuesday of the next week, we received the first good news since Rena's illness. The new chemo treatments were working.

That was last August. Today, seven months later, my niece, Rena Giovanni, is in full remission.

Was it divine intervention? A blessing from above? A miracle?

I have one word for the nonbelievers: Absolutely!

Joe T.

This is a true story that happened to me when I was living abroad. No matter what religion you may be, I would like to share my story with you about my miraculous experience.

On February 17, 2004, my cousin and I went to church to pray for our friend, who had recently been in an automobile accident. I had not been to church in several months and, to tell you the truth, I have never been big on prayer. Our friend was in a coma, though, and I felt desperate.

When we entered the church, we immediately noticed two candles burning brightly at the front of the church. I guess we were drawn to them because the church was very dark except for the two flames illuminating the altar.

We prayed for about twenty minutes and then decided to kneel at the altar and say a final prayer together before leaving for the hospital. As we approached the altar, though, we both stopped in our tracks. We stood there frozen, open-mouthed and wide-eyed. We looked at each other and then again at the candles.

"Do you see it too?" I asked Jana, as we dared not move.

"Oh, my Lord," she responded. What we saw was that

both candles were melting in the shape of the Virgin Mary. As we watched in silence, we noticed that the shapes were becoming more and more obvious. And although both shapes were in the form of Mary, they were very different.

One candle looked like a profile of Mary, a long slender figure with a flowing gown and a rosary in her hand. We could see what looked like a round face slightly bent forward.

The other candle also took the shape of Our Lady but this one seemed to be more of a back view of a robe that fell in several folds. We could definitely see the figure of a woman, but her face seemed to be hidden by a veil.

I am a professional photographer by nature, so my first instinct was to run to my car for my camera. As I walked toward the candles with my camera, I saw the shapes of Mary very clearly, and yet I also noticed the statues behind the altar. I couldn't help but notice that the two candles were exactly in the shape of the two statues that were behind the altar.

My cousin and I were astounded by the whole event and ended up staying at the church for two hours.

Afterwards, on the ride to the hospital, neither of us spoke. I suppose we were trying to absorb and process the

CHERI LOMONTE
THE BLUE CARVED MADONNA

unbelievable experience.

We arrived at the hospital at 8:05 p.m., drained and barely able to move. But as we checked in at the nurse's station, we were surprised to find that our friend had been moved from ICU. She was no longer in critical condition. In fact, we later found out, she had miraculously gained consciousness and might be leaving the hospital in a few days.

Well, as I said before, I have never been big on prayer. But that is certainly in the past, because now I truly am a believer. I have been enlightened by the Mother of God and know that prayer does, in fact, work.

Anonymous

It's hot, dusty and dry in Egypt. The sun does nothing but shine, beating down incessantly on one's head and shoulders, burning, searing. I don't know exactly what it was that took me into the small church. I'm not Catholic but something drew me inside. Perhaps the cool darkness? A need for quiet?

When I first went in, I lit a candle and started to move to take a seat. Before I knew it, a woman attired in local dress instructed her young son to go up and knock my candle over. I don't know if she was angry with me because I'm an American or what, but it was certainly an act of aggression and disrespect. It disturbed me and I considered leaving, but continued on to kneel and pray.

As I prayed, I saw a beautiful vision of Mary. It was blue and I just stayed with it for a while and then it slowly disappeared. It gave me a feeling of such incredible peace, a true sense that Mary was in that place. It was a peace that I needed at the time, because I was going through a divorce. It was one of those visions that just take you into it. I got so excited when I realized what was happening that I took myself out of the experience a little bit, but the feeling has certainly stayed with me.

Later, when I was sharing the experience with a friend, I was told that Mary had appeared in that area regularly and that the church had been built especially for Her. It is interesting to think about the fact that Mary and Joseph had hidden from the Romans fairly close by shortly after Jesus had been born. I also later wondered if maybe Mary wanted me to feel comfortable in her church, even after the boy had been rude, and that perhaps her appearance was a gift of welcome and comfort.

But the most wonderful thing about the entire experience is the fact that I can go back to that "place" of peace when I need it, just by remembering her image.

Patricia S.

I had a true miracle occur with Lourdes water. I fell from a moving truck and badly damaged my right knee. I managed to get to the house and by that time my knee was three times its normal size. I started applying the water and praying. Two hours later it was normal size again. Mary is so blessed. She is always there for me.

C.K., Kansas

It was the most disgusting sight anyone had ever seen. About one and a half inches in diameter, the open sore would redden, ooze, dry up, and then start the process all over again.

For eighteen months, I endured the pain and frustration of over a hundred doctor visits, but to no avail. No one could tell me the cause, no one could heal my sore—until the good doctor, Dr. Joseph Morgan, told me that he might be able to help.

"But you'll have to help too, Anne," he said. "You'll have to pray extra hard, and you'll have to believe."

And I'll never forget his words of wisdom—wisdom that I had never before heard from a doctor.

"I am a man of medicine, but I am only a man," he said. "You must ask for help from above."

After all the doctors and all the hospital visits, no one had ever mentioned prayer. Why not, I thought. Nothing else has worked.

So I began to pray…and pray…and pray. I prayed to the Blessed Mother in particular because she was always the one I turned to in times of despair. After all, a very warm and nurturing mother who had taught me the importance of

99

honoring Mary, the Virgin Mother of God, had raised me.

On March 3, 2003, I met with Dr. Morgan and he told me that he wanted to try a new, anti-inflammatory drug and, if I was willing to be a guinea pig, he was willing to test it on me. This would be the ninth drug in eighteen months. Again, I was tired and disgusted by the deepening wound and agreed to try it. Why not, I again thought.

On March 15 I met the young nurses who would be responsible for cleaning and dressing my wound on a weekly basis. Suzie was about twenty-four and Mary Beth, not much older. They were sweet and kind, and I had a good feeling about the whole process. And on this day, I also began my oral anti-inflammatory drugs. Dr. Morgan told me that it would take about six weeks to see any results. He told me that we were praying for new tissue growth and at each visit, that is the first thing they would check.

I went home a bit hopeful and a bit skeptical, but nevertheless I followed Dr. Morgan's instructions: take my medicine as prescribed and pray.

On March 22, one week later, I went in for my second treatment. The sore was no longer hurting and the redness had subsided.

But when my young friends came in to clean and dress

the wound, they began to giggle.

"What's going on, girls?" I asked hesitantly. They told me to wait and that they would return in a minute.

To my surprise they returned with Dr. Morgan, whose eyes immediately found the sore.

"Yes, girls, you're right," he nodded. And then he turned to me, put his warm hand on my cold hand, and smiled.

"Anne, dear, you must be praying because what usually takes six weeks has only taken one. We see here that new flesh is growing. It is paper thin, but it is growing. And that means, dear, that you are on the road to recovery."

I couldn't believe my ears. It couldn't be. It had been over eighteen months of pain and agony.

Some people might say it was the medicine that did it, and they may be right. But I know in my heart that it wasn't only the medicine that ultimately cured me. I know that it was some force greater than we can ever imagine. And everyday I thank that force—the Blessed Mother of God—for hearing me and answering my desperate prayers.

Anne K.

ome people say it is a gift, some say it is a curse. But I don't really mind the fact that strangers feel the need to speak to me about personal matters.

My name is Connie and I have always had a special devotion to Our Lady. In fact, I own a gift shop near the cathedral in Santa Fe, New Mexico that specializes in medals and rosaries and special prayers to Mary, Mother of God.

I see lots of people from all walks of life, so when this woman walked into my shop, I didn't pay too much attention. Her bright red suit and stylish pumps suggested that she was definitely a stranger in town. And her newly styled hair was a giveaway that she had just come from a hair salon. I thought she was an attractive young woman, but her nervousness seemed to wear on her.

I saw her fidgeting with the new rosaries I had just received and then I watched as she tossed them down roughly and rushed over to the medals. She didn't seem the type to steal, but I became suspicious when I noticed that she kept looking over her shoulder at me.

When I asked if she needed any help, she bounded over to me, slammed her Gucci purse on the counter, and blurted, "Oh yes, I certainly need lots of help, if I may ask. Can you please tell me where I can find a psychic. My ex-husband is trying to rob me of all of my inheritance, and our court appearance is in two hours."

I patted her soft, warm hands that were now pressed into the counter in desperation.

"Honey," I said. "You don't need a psychic. In fact, I'll tell you exactly what you need.

"Here's what you do. Go down to the cathedral and on the north side you will see La Conquistadora's Chapel. Kneel in front of her and tell her what you need. Pray and tell her that I sent you. She knows me well. That's really all you need, dear."

She thanked me, rushed off, and as she slammed the door behind her, I yelled, "I'll pray for you too." I'm not sure that she heard me, but I do know that she listened. Because about three hours later, as I was closing up my shop, the pretty lady with the red suit came rushing back and in her hand were a dozen roses.

She offered me the roses and smiled, "I did everything that you told me. And guess what, I came out smelling like a rose in court."

"Oh, I am so glad. I knew that she would help you," I

104

said. "And thank you so much for the beautiful roses, dear. What a thoughtful gift!"

"Oh, no," she smiled again and this time I felt her soft warm hands grab my old wrinkly ones. "It is I who must thank you. For you have given me a gift much greater than any I have ever received before. You have given me the gift of faith for I truly believe that La Conquistadora was responsible for my triumph today. I will be forever grateful to you both."

And how odd, I thought, after the shop door slammed for a second time that day. I didn't even find out her name.

Connie H.

Recently I had a circulatory problem in my right carotid artery and had only ten percent circulation from a severe blockage and could have had a stroke. I needed surgery. I used Lourdes water on my neck and prayed that I would not have a stroke before or during surgery. My prayers were answered and I am now recovering.

E.M., Rhode Island

CHERI LOMONTE
A CROWN FOR MARY

y mother died when I was two years old. Of course I don't remember her death, but what I do remember are the long, tearful nights crying for her. I remember waking up in the dark, sweat drenching my hair, and salty tears forming at the corners of my mouth. I remember asking God why—why me? Why did I have to be the one without a mother? Why did I have to wipe away my own tears? Why didn't He take someone else's mother instead of mine?

I always felt sad and different because I didn't have a mother, but never so sad as on my first day of grade school when all the mothers hugged and kissed their cherubs goodbye while I stood alone, watching and longing for the warmth of a mother's embrace. I remember thinking that it wasn't fair that I, a mere six year old, should be so alone and so deserted. Oh, how I longed for a mother in those days.

And later, when I was thirteen, I remember running away to my uncle's cabin in the woods. Could it be that I could die out there alone and no one would even miss me? No mother to weep over my grave? Yes, I suppose I was rather dramatic but what thirteen year old isn't? So I spent the night there alone, unsure why I was even there.

When I heard the first rustling outside the door was the

106

time I started praying. I had never really prayed before, and I was still pretty angry with a God who stole my mother, so I prayed to Mary.

My grandmother always made me go to church, so it's not like I didn't know the prayers. I knew them, all right. So I prayed and prayed and prayed. I remember the terror I felt as the rustling turned into growling and then something scratching on the cabin door. I had heard about Old Sam from my uncle, but I had always thought it was just a story. Old Sam, the grizzly, was just a legend, wasn't he?

I must have said at least two hundred Hail Mary's that night. And I promised the Blessed Mother that if I made it through the night, I would be forever devoted to her. Well, I did make it through the night and emerged from that cabin with a new purpose in life—to love and serve Mary, Mother of God.

My name is Adolfo M., and I am a composer. I have never had any formal music education, but somehow I have managed to write over four-hundred-fifty songs, all in honor of the Blessed Mother. Ever since that night when Mary saved my life, I have been composing music and have managed to share my devotional hymns with millions of people.

In fact, some people have said that one of my songs, "O Virgin Conquistador," was directly responsible for a miracle. I was on my way back from Albuquerque, New Mexico when, on a whim, I decided to stop in Santa Fe. I immediately knew something unusual was going on there when I discovered a procession of woman and children, all wearing drab brown dresses and carrying tiny gold crowns. I remember thinking that they looked so sad as they trudged through the streets with their heads hanging low.

I asked a stranger what was going on and he told me that the statue of the Blessed Mother, the oldest statue of the Madonna in the continental United States, had recently been stolen from the cathedral. I knew then that my visit to Santa Fe had not been an accident. Mary had brought me there for a reason and the reason was a song. In a matter of minutes, I had written "O Virgin Conquistador." In a matter of hours, the statue of the Blessed Mother had been found. As I get older, I continue to write songs for Mary. I continue to thank her for all that she has done for me. And most of all, I continue to honor the Blessed Mother for saving me and giving my life purpose and being my true, heavenly mother.

Adolfo M.

ctober 12, 1987, is a day I will never forget. My husband and I and our three children had just moved to Portugal. My son, Adam, a normal seventeen year old, came home from a rock concert with an unusually high temperature—we had not even had time to find a doctor, so I was a bit concerned when I had to settle for the only doctor on call that night. Dr. Borges was his name, and he immediately diagnosed Adam with a urine infection. He gave him the appropriate medication and told us that the fever should subside within a few hours. After a few days however, Adam's fever remained high. We again brought Adam in and this time we saw Dr. Mangus, who took an x-ray and diagnosed Adam with pneumonia. And again, Adam was given more medication.

October 16 rolled around and still Adam was not improving. Dr. Crowley this time suggested that Adam should stay the night at the hospital for more testing. The hospital was a nightmare. After fighting for a private room, I soon learned that Adam's room had recently been sprayed for mosquitoes. I was appalled. My poor ailing son now had to deal with dangerous bug spray.

October 17 would be a better day, or so I thought. But

as I walked into his room that morning I knew something was terribly wrong. Adam looked pale and seemed lethargic. He was beginning to slur his words and even drifted off to sleep in mid-sentence. I immediately called the nurse, who said that the results of his blood tests were in—everything was normal. I was enraged. "Look at him," I screamed, "Does he look normal to you?"

October 18 wasn't much better. Adam broke out in red blotches, and the doctors were quick to diagnose him with measles. I was suspicious. I had had measles as a child; this was not measles. I called in Dr. Crowley, who did more testing and admitted that I was right—this was definitely not measles. He suggested that we take Adam to the Coimbra University Research Hospital—the best hospital in Portugal, so they said. And yes, I was skeptical.

It was in Coimbra that I started to pray. The doctors told us that Adam was bleeding to death internally. They gave him a plasma transfusion and placed him on ice. I hurried to the hospital's chapel and prayed to Our Lady of Fatima. For the next six weeks, while Adam remained at Coimbra, I prayed like I had never prayed before. But nothing seemed to change.

December 3 had arrived, and now the doctors were

111

suggesting that we move Adam to the United States. We arranged for him to be admitted to Yale New Haven Hospital and arrived there on December 8. My spirits were low but my hopes were high. I continued to pray.

December 12 was not a good day. Several doctors arrived in Adam's room that morning and told us that they had never seen anything like this before. Adam was not responding to antibiotics and his condition was worsening. They were clueless. I was terrified. I felt Adam slipping away, and I knew that something had to be done. Someone, somewhere must be able to help him. I continued to pray and pray and pray.

December 20, five days before Christmas, the doctors told us that our other children should be tested as donors. Adam's only chance at survival was a bone marrow transplant. And although we were devastated, I knew what to do. I kissed Adam's sweaty forehead as he lay sleeping on the immaculately white hospital bed and headed for the chapel. This time I prayed that if Our Lady of Fatima cured my son, I would walk from my hometown in Portugal to Fatima. I had never walked more than a couple of miles, yet I vowed that I would fulfill the journey in honor of her.

December 22, and I awoke with a stiff neck after

112

spending the night on the hospital couch. I wanted to be next to Adam all night, in case he needed me, or as I look back now, because I needed him. I needed to hear his breathing as I had done so many years before when I would creep into the nursery to make sure my beautiful baby boy's chest was moving, taking in and letting out air. Yes, he's alive and breathing, I thought as I touched his chest and looked at his calm face. But something seemed different that morning. His face had color, his skin was clear, his chest was warm, and his breathing regular. Adam opened his eyes and looked at me. He sat up and started to speak like he had on October 11. He seemed normal, but it must be my imagination, I thought.

December 23 was a glorious day. The doctors told us that Adam's white blood cell count was returning to normal. They called off the blood transfusion, and told us that Adam's siblings may not need to be tested for the bone marrow transplant. We would all hold our breaths; we would wait and see.

December 25 was more than glorious—it was miraculous. Adam's white blood cell count was normal, his fever was down, and he was eating like a horse. The doctors told us that we could take Adam home. They could not explain it, but he was cured. We didn't need presents that Christmas. Our Christmas miracle was Adam, and we had Our Lady of Fatima to thank for it.

And thank her I did. It took me three years to get back to Portugal to fulfill my promise, but I did it. I completed the journey to Fatima, thanking Our Lady every step of the way—for her help, for our family, and especially for our dear Adam.

And speaking of Adam, today he is the proud father of two healthy sons and one beautiful daughter. He has never been ill since that awful winter of 1987, and each day we all give thanks to Our Lady of Fatima who blessed us and gave him back to us.

A Family Story, Christina N.

Do you have a story about Mary?

I invite you to share with others your prayers, poems, and stories of intercessory miracles.

Send your submissions to me for inclusion in the next edition of *The Healing Touch of Mary*.

Email me at Stories@divineimpressions.com

If you have questions, or would like to *tell* me your story, call me at (800) 682 1729.

All net proceeds from the books will be given to charities.

Thank you,
Cheri Lomonte

It was Father Michael W. who encouraged my artwork, but it was Father Mullen who taught me how to pray. He was the one who told me to be myself and just ask the Blessed Mother for the relationship that I had never had with her but secretly always wanted. It seemed too easy, but I told him I would give it a try.

I had been preparing my artwork of the Blessed Mother for several months but had felt all along that something wasn't quite working. As I was organizing my work for the church art show late one October night, I decided to try saying the rosary. I hadn't said a rosary in twenty years, but in a strange way, something seemed to tell me to do so now. I said the rosary and then proceeded to ask the Blessed Mother for guidance and reassurance. I remember feeling unusually calm and thinking how happy I was that the bright light that usually beams into our living room from the alley was out. I could relax and enjoy the moonlight. And as cliché as this may sound, as soon as I had these thoughts, the light came on. Or rather, a new kind of light, and now it was beginning to glow.

I could not keep my eyes off of the light and felt mesmerized as it got brighter and brighter until I had to turn

118

Holy Mary

away. As if I was not shocked enough, as I turned away, I noticed that my computer light and VCR light were pulsating. It couldn't be happening to me!

But it was happening, and as I placed the rosary on my coffee table and attempted to rise, the bright light went out, the pulsating ceased, and I truly felt a sense of complete calm.

Well, of course my wife thought I just needed sleep and, until this day, I wonder if it really happened. All I truly know is that the next morning I woke with a clear vision—almost a blueprint, in fact—of my art show. I knew exactly how to marry the old images of Mary with the new and how to organize them so that the entire world could see her majesty. I didn't tell my wife until months later, I suppose because it hadn't occurred to me then, but I had been praying the Luminous Mysteries. I had been praying for inspiration and enlightenment, and that is exactly what I got on that crisp autumn night.

Cristian W.

120

As a Eucharistic minister I was taking communion to a shut-in. The lady I visited was living with her daughter while in her last stages of suffering from lung cancer. She had a gorgeous rosary hanging beside her bed. During my visits we started saying the rosary. Besides my Sunday visits I started visiting once during the week, always ending our time together with a rosary and talking about the Blessed Mother.

Her daughter called me one day and told me her mother had taken a turn for the worse, she had been hospitalized. Would I visit her in the hospital? Of course I went immediately and sat by my friend's bedside. We started our time together by saying the rosary. The whole time she kept her eyes over my right shoulder to the point where I turned around to see if anyone was there. I didn't see anyone and we continued until she fell asleep. I left quietly after I whispered in her ear that I would be back Friday.

On Friday I found her much worse but she greeted me and asked me where the lady was that I had brought with me on my last visit. She was so beautiful, she said. Was she my sister? I asked her what she looked like. Between gasping for breath she went on to describe the Blessed Mother.

Her daughter called me that night to tell me her mother had passed away.

Joan M.

FATHER WILLIAM HART MCNICHOLS
THE BLACK MADONNA

121

y daughter Anne is a very strong woman, so when she gave birth to her second child, Hannah, by caesarian section I was not surprised to find that she only stayed in the hospital for two days. I learned later though that the doctors only released her early because she had been so insistent. I guess Anne had always been a strong-willed child, and I always admired her for that, but I also knew that her obstinacy would one day get her in real trouble.

And that day was Sunday, May 10. My son-in-law was concerned because Anne had fainted at mass that morning. I had never worried about Anne in my life, and this time was no different. But when Jonathan called back at 7:15 Monday morning to say that Anne was asking for me, I knew that something was not right. I told him that I would be over in the evening, after work, and to call if he needed me before then. I said a prayer to the Blessed Mother to keep Anne safe and to watch over her until I could get there.

But something I call miraculous happened at about 8:45 that morning. I was on my way to work, headed up Grant Street, one block away from work when I heard a strange voice. At first I thought it was on the radio, so I turned the radio off and continued on my way. A few seconds later, though, I heard the voice again.

"GO NOW!" the voice whispered.

I immediately pulled over to the side of the road, shaken and confused. And then I heard it again—and again, the same two words:

"GO NOW!"

I closed my eyes, rested my head against the seat, and prayed that I was not having an aneurysm. But another strange thing happened when I opened my eyes. There in front of me was a billboard advertising the local news station, Channel Four News with Anne Montgomery. And the name ANNE seemed surrounded by a halo of purple light.

I immediately knew the message was to get to my daughter and to get to her fast. I turned my car around and headed south. When I arrived, Anne was in bed. I took one look at her and knew that something was terribly wrong. She was jaundiced and barely able to move. And when Anne agreed to go to the hospital without an iota of an argument, I knew it was the right decision. I immediately called the hospital, doctor, and Jonathan to say that I was bringing Anne in right away.

When we arrived at St. Joseph's, the doctor took one look at her and starting barking orders. And before I knew it, what seemed like twenty staff members came out of nowhere with tubes and syringes and bags with clear liquids attached to poles. I was given orders to wait in Room 1-A

Room 1-A was a sparse, cold, green-colored room with a rollaway hospital bed in one corner of the room. There were no chairs in the room so my choices were to sit on the hospital bed or stand. So I stood. And I paced. And I leaned on the wall. And I paced, until finally I could take it no longer—I had to find out about my Anne.

The nurse's station was busy, so I decided to look around a bit. But before I could take two steps, I ran right into the doctor in charge.

"I was wondering where you were," he said.

"I am Dr. Savitor and I have some news. Your daughter is going to be fine, thanks to you. Her blood count should be 37 and, when she was admitted, it was 14. We have found that she has a severe form of anemia and have given her several pints of blood."

And before I could speak, Dr. Savitor patted me on the back and smiled. "She'll be O.K., but you really have saved her life. You brought her in at 9:30. If you had brought her

in two hours later, she would not be with us today."

I was shocked. And then I remembered the voice that had told me to "GO NOW," and I knew that the voice that I heard could be none other than the Blessed Mother telling me to go and save my daughter.

David M.

Having been sick and away from my postal job for several weeks, I made a visit to say hello to my friends. While making my rounds I came upon a friend whose face was so distorted that he could not close his right eye and had to talk out of the side of his mouth. I asked him what happened and he mumbled it was some kind of stroke. I went home and found the bottle of Lourdes water and gave it to Phil the next morning. I counseled him that it was not a drugstore prescription—that prayer from the heart to Mary with its use was necessary. The next morning I went to the post office and three people told me that Phil was looking for me. When I found him, he was completely cured—not a twitch, his eye was normal and speech clear. He said to me, "God Bless you." Some people don't believe in miracles, but I do. I had just witnessed a very personal miracle.

A.C., Maine

hen I heard that I had missed the apparition, I was heartbroken. Yes, I was visiting Ivan Abshire's farm to hear confessions from the many faithful who had gathered there, but like them, I also was hoping to see Our Lady herself.

But she had chosen to reveal herself to only one person, Laura Mary Greerson. Laura told me that as Our Lady appeared, so did hundreds and hundreds of roses. The roses were red and yellow and pink and were spread all around Mary's feet. At one point the roses seemed to cover Mary and then they disappeared altogether.

I found myself mesmerized by Laura's story, but not so mesmerized as when she told me that Mary had said that the roses were for me.

"You must have heard wrong," I replied.

"Father Julio," Laura said, looking me in the eye, "no, Father, with all due respect, I know what I heard, and I heard that the flowers were for you."

Needless to say, I did not sleep well that night. I kept wondering if it was true, if Laura was right, if Mary, Mother of God, was offering me roses. I felt surprised and especially humbled. And I also felt a bit guilty for questioning Laura's words.

127

The next day, though, I returned to the farm and instead of hearing confession right away as I had been doing for the last three days, I decided to give an impromptu mass. I'm not sure why, but something seemed to be telling me to consecrate the scene with a mass.

It was an ordinary mass—at first. But as I was about to begin my sermon, the smell of roses began to waft through the air. At first it was a vague, sweet scent and then it began to intensify until it was so strong that it seemed to hypnotize the crowd. I can only describe it as if the roses were a liquid drenching the people—a deluge of scents pouring on and on.

And then as I tried to go on, I noticed what looked like glitter sprinkled over my sermon notes. I looked around, trying to find the source while remaining in control. I saw the makeshift altar and the same glitter material adorning the communion cloth.

In my moment of indecision—whether to go on as planned or speak to the strange happenings—a young boy of about fifteen appeared out of nowhere and asked if I would bless the roses that he had with him. He told me that they were for his mother whose arthritis was so debilitating that she could no longer get out of bed.

Needless to say, I did not continue with my plan but instead continued with what could only be Our Lady's plan. I called on anyone who would like roses to be blessed and all of a sudden, people were coming to me in droves to bless their roses. I never knew where they were coming from or how the people just happened to have roses with them on that day, but I continued to bless the red and yellow and pink roses.

And as the months went by, I continued to receive letters from people who said that the roses that I had blessed on that day had been responsible for healings. I especially have kept the letter of Jose Rondeto, the fifteen-year-old boy whose mother is now free of arthritis.

Father Julio R.

Sometimes when I am alone with her, it seems like her expressions change. It is almost as if she were not a statue, but a real person instead. Some people think I am imagining things, and maybe I am, but I could swear on a million Bibles that I have seen La Conquistadora sad, happy, serious, and even playful.

I began my duties as the sacristiana of La Conquistadora several years ago when my friend Connie became ill. When she asked me if I would take over for her, I was petrified. Yes, I was definitely petrified, but I knew I had to do it. It almost seemed that I was being called, and although I knew that taking care of the sacristy would require many hours on my part, I also knew that I could handle the responsibility.

In addition to cleaning the altar and making sure the candles stay lit continually, I also am responsible for dressing La Conquistadora. A typical outfit will consist of the gown itself, her crown and scepter, and her jewelry.

It always is a spiritual experience for me because as I dress La Conquistadora, I pray. I pray for myself, my friends, my family, and even for strangers. On one particular occasion, a strange thing happened when I was praying for my sister who was about to be married.

I had decided to do my duties early that morning so that I would have the rest of the day to help my sister with her last minute wedding plans. It was three weeks before Christmas and time to dress La Conquistadora in the gold and purple Christmas gown she always wore for the Christmas season.

At first I thought that perhaps my mind wasn't on the task—perhaps I had been thinking too much of Irene and Adolpho. But forty-five minutes into the dressing, I realized that something was not right. Could the dress be different somehow? But that didn't make sense, because I was the only one who had the key to her wardrobe closet. And this was the third year I had dressed La Conquistadora in this outfit, so I would know if something was different.

So I kept trying and trying. The dress just wouldn't fit. When I noticed that I had been trying to make the dress fit for two hours, I gave up. No way was this dress going to fit on La Conquistadora. As I went to the closet to return the dress, the first thing that I saw was Our Lady's white birthday dress. I don't know what possessed me, but I gently took the dress off of the hanger and headed back to try again.

The delicate, lacey white gown trimmed in pearls and

132

baby roses slid on beautifully. And as I stepped back to look, a tear ran down my face. This elegant, pure, and yet simple white dress was almost the exact replica of my sister Irene's wedding dress.

Perhaps it was coincidence, but I choose to believe otherwise. Somehow I know in my heart that Our Lady was trying to tell me that my prayers would be answered. That was many years ago, and I am happy to report that Irene and Adolpho will celebrate their twentieth wedding anniversary this December.

133

Emelda M.

I had recently moved to Calgary when a woman I met at church asked me if I would drive her to Denver, Colorado because she had heard about Our Lady appearing to a woman there. Well, as you can expect, I thought she was insane. For one, I did not know this woman from Adam, and for two, I did not believe in apparitions and supernatural happenings.

That night, however, I had a dream about this woman. In the dream, we were on a mountaintop, surrounded by children, overlooking a city. At first it disturbed me, but I quickly forgot about it until several days later when I literally ran into this woman at the supermarket. We both stopped short to stare at each other. Both of us held a bunch of roses with baby's breath and a white ribbon tied around the bottom. We looked at each other and then at the identical rose bouquets with the stickers on the cellophane that said $14.99.

She introduced herself as May Martin, and then she proceeded to tell me about herself. I learned that we lived in the same neighborhood and had children exactly the same age. We talked for a few minutes and then, as she turned to go, she pointed the bouquet at me and said, "Don't forget about Denver."

I told my husband about May Martin, the odd request, the dream, and the chance meeting. My very logical, rational, engineer husband, of course, said one word, "Coincidence." I too am a very grounded and rational person and agreed instantly with his assessment.

But something kept gnawing at me that I could not explain. I could not get this woman off of my mind. And then, about three days later, when I least expected it, I saw her again. This time it was in the doctor's office. I was sitting reading an interesting article on heart imaging in the latest *Time* when I felt a tap on my shoulder.

"Hi, Edna," she said, and sat next to me. That was when I knew that this was no coincidence. Someone or something was trying to bring us together. And before I knew it, I was offering to drive her to Denver.

We arrived in Denver on May 15, 1992. After checking into the hotel, May decided to take a nap and I decided to go to mass at St. Thomas More.

As I arrived, I saw people heading into a hall where a young girl was already giving a talk. Every seat was taken and people were standing against the walls and sitting on the floor. I snuck down the side to join those on the floor when a lady caught my eye and beckoned me to the empty seat next to her. I couldn't believe my eyes—an empty seat? I thanked her and when I asked the name of the speaker, she looked at me as if I was from Mars.

"Of course that is Teresa," she said, and nodded as if I was supposed to know this girl. She then introduced herself as Veronica and shared her prayer sheet with me. Veronica had a string of beads in her hand and, as we finished the prayer, she opened my hand and gently placed it in, saying, "Our Lady wants you to have this!"

136

Strangely, in my other hand I had a small wooden cross that I never normally carried. A monk at the Holy Shrine of Our Lord in Jerusalem had given it to me. I placed it in Veronica's hand and she smiled.

When Teresa finished her speech, people started crowding around my new friend Veronica. They started to snap pictures and, as I leaned to avoid the photos, Veronica pulled me back in and said, "Stay, please, they think you are my mother."

I was so confused at the time, but later I was to discover that Veronica was the woman who May had first told me about. She was the woman to whom the Blessed Mother had been appearing. When I discovered this I knew that my

FATHER WILLIAM HART MCNICHOLS
MOTHER OF GOD

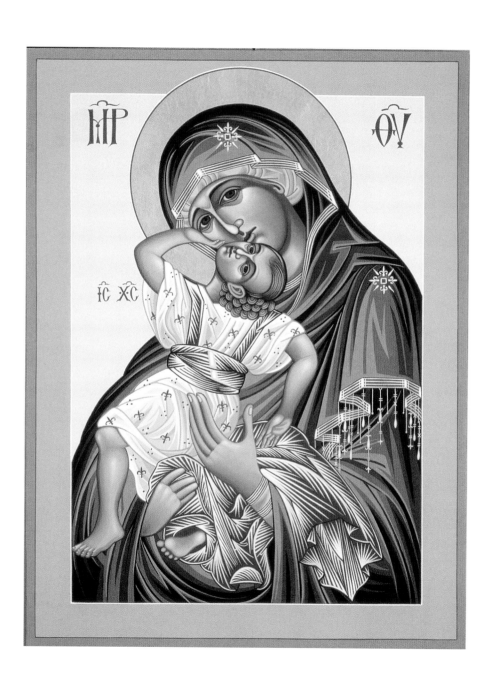

137

visit to Denver had been planned all along. And since then I have realized that not everything can be rationalized. Sometimes you just have to follow your intuition.

Since my experience with Veronica, I have listened more to my heart and followed my intuition. In fact, I have recently been in charge of organizing pilgrimage groups to Denver and have met hundreds of wonderful people. I guess I never believed people when they would say something was their "calling." But now I do. I truly believe that all people are called. Although sometimes they have to be called and called and called again!

138

Edna M.

ver since I can remember, I have had a special devotion to Our Lady. My mother says it all started on my fifth birthday when the "best birthday party ever" turned into the "biggest disaster ever." It was three weeks after her mother had passed away, and she reminded me that she was trying to celebrate my life as well as cheer herself up.

But everything that could go wrong did go wrong. From the burnt cake to the torrential rain to the fight between Sergio and Peter, nothing seemed to go right. Interestingly though, the only memory I have of that day was when my friends left and my mother and I drove over to church to put flowers at Our Lady's feet. It was then that my mother informed me that the mother of Baby Jesus and I shared the same birthday. I remember thinking at the time that I was the most special person in the world.

That was a long time ago, but ever since then, I have been visiting Our Lady on our birthday and placing roses at her feet.

Yes, it has always been a tradition for me, but last September 8 was different. I remember placing the baby roses at Our Lady's statue, saying a prayer of devotion to her, and then leaving for home. It was afternoon by then

140

and I remember thinking how odd it was that my boys had not called to wish me a happy birthday. And later as I was preparing to go out to dinner with my husband, I again realized that the kids had not called. How odd, I thought. They never forget my birthday.

So when the phone rang a few minutes later, I jumped. Oh, one of the boys remembered, I thought. But the voice on the other end of the line was not one of my sons. In fact, it was a female's voice.

"Mrs. D," she said, "I want to congratulate you. It seems that your name was picked for our yearly trip giveaway. And you have won a trip to wherever you would like to go." Of course I thought it was a telemarketer, or someone playing a birthday joke on me. But it turned out to be real. My husband informed me that he had filled out an entry form at Worldwide Travel Agency a few months before for their yearly summer travel giveaway.

Well, I chose to go to Medjugorje and, believe me, the first thing I did when I arrived was to thank Mary, Mother of Baby Jesus, for the very special and very wonderful birthday present that she gave to me on September 8, 2003.

Lilly D.

FATHER WILLIAM HART MCNICHOLS
OUR LADY OF THE NEW ADVENT

I was diagnosed with leukemia in 1989, and made my first trip to Medjugorje in 1990. I would like to tell you that I have been cured, but I cannot. That is not my story.

What I would like to tell you, though, is about my devotion to Mary, Mother of God. When I was five years old, my family moved to Santa Fe, New Mexico. If you know anything about Santa Fe, you know that the people are very devoted to La Conquistadora. I suppose that is where my faith started as well.

When I was little, my grandmother taught the catechism of Catholicism to me. She never lectured but instead reminded me that La Conquistadora would always be there if I needed her. Every year we participated in the procession in honor of Our Lady and continued with the nine-day novena.

After my marriage though, everything changed. I always thought that Santa Fe was the best place in the world, and I often told my family that I could never imagine leaving it. But I met my husband in the summer of 1971, and of course, being in the military, he was transferred overseas. I would have to leave my heaven on earth.

So I concocted a plan—a plan that lasted over twenty

FATHER WILLIAM HART McNICHOLS
OUR LADY OF THE SANDIAS

143

years. I decided that while I was away, I would become a seamstress for La Conquistadora. I had been a friend of the sacristiana of the cathedral, so I made sure that she gave me accurate measurements. And I began to sew.

We traveled to Germany and I sewed a gown made of the finest navy blue velvet that Germany produced. We traveled to Italy and I made a green and yellow dress made of soft satin fibers. We traveled to Africa and I made her a Christmas dress of gold and white with tiny diamonds sewn into the collar. And my sewing continued as we traveled the world.

144

In 1989 when my doctor told me that I had cancer, I prayed to Mary for guidance. I prayed that she might help me to cope, and I promised that no matter what happened, I would always be grateful to her for my special life.

In 1990 when I returned from Medjugorje, my doctor told me I was improving tremendously. In fact, he wanted to know what I had been doing differently because my cancer had gone into remission.

Well, I cannot say that I am totally cured because you never know when that ugly thing called cancer will rear its head again, but I do know that I will never be afraid as long as La Conquistadora is my guide.

Mary A.

It was Italian night again on our street. I loved my neighbors, and I especially loved our Italian night get-togethers because of the fabulous food and relaxed atmosphere. But this night felt different and the feeling intensified the minute I crossed Bonnie Savelli's threshold.

An older woman, someone I didn't know, met me at the door. Instead of the usual introductions one would expect, she grasped my hand and asked, "Are you Catholic?"

And even before I could answer, she said, "Look, I need healing water from Lourdes. Can you get that for me? I'm Jewish, I believe in miracles—and I'm desperate."

I don't know what possessed me, but I immediately responded, "Oh yes, I can do that."

In fact, I had no idea how I would do that. But after listening to her story about her grandson who had recently been born with physical defects, I again said, "No problem, I'll have that for you next week." I also remember thinking to myself that I had lost my mind. Why was I lying to this poor old woman? And how would she feel when I let her down?

At mass the next day, when Father Michael asked that special intentions be requested aloud, I blurted out that I

needed healing water from Lourdes. As I was leaving church a few minutes later, a man tapped me on the shoulder and said, " I have healing water from Lourdes that you may have. My brother just returned from there, and I would be happy to share it with you.

Whenever I need something special, or whenever I need something that seems impossible, I always ask Our Blessed Mother to intercede, and she always seems to grant my requests.

And this time was no different.

Cheri Lomonte

147

I am eighty-six years old and I have had polio since 1928. I recently had a stroke and I am now in a wheelchair twenty-four hours a day. My legs developed open sores and would not heal. I put Lourdes water on my legs every day and the sores healed.

F.J., California

148

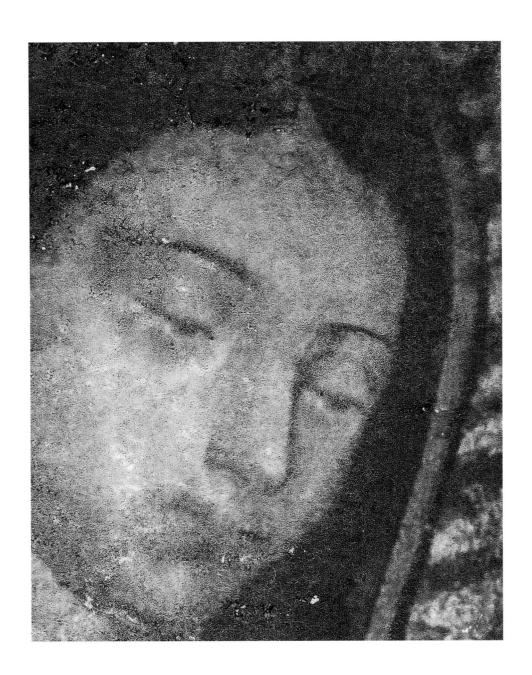

She can help you if you pray to her," I told my almost six-year-old son Anthony. It was May 11, 1998, and we were standing in front of a statue of the Blessed Mother in our church. Anthony's small voice recited the "Hail Mary" as I prayed a "Hail Mary" in silence with tears running down my cheeks.

The tears were with good reason. Almost two years before, Anthony had been diagnosed with a disease that had no known cure. He was so young, so hopeful, and I wanted so much to help him.

This disease, a debilitating form of arthritis, had taken over much of his body and he often ran high fevers and was anemic. Sometimes Anthony was unable to walk at all from the swelling and pain in his ankles and at other times he limped from the pain in his hip.

To my surprise, four days after we had said our "Hail Marys" a box arrived in the mail from the Lourdes Center in Boston with six bottles of Lourdes water. I had no idea who had requested that it be sent, but it was postmarked on the very day that we had said our "Hail Marys"! Was this the answer to our prayers?

A few days later, I watched with an overwhelming

149

feeling of hope as Anthony and his brother Francis poured Lourdes water over each of Anthony's joints, praying a "Hail Mary" for each joint. Anthony immediately began to be cured of his incurable disease. Within two weeks he was no longer anemic and within a year and a half, he was off all medications. Finally, in April of 2002 our prayers were answered—in a letter written by his physician, Anthony was declared "free of arthritis."

On May 11, 2002, Anthony walked down the aisle to receive his First Holy Communion. I reminded Anthony of the May 11th four years earlier when we had said our "Hail Marys" and the Lourdes water had been mailed. With the complete faith in miracles and trust of a child, Anthony said matter-of-factly, "Mary probably had it all planned out."

Paula L., Anthony's Mother

The rosaries were all gone. I had been waiting patiently for over an hour. And now when it was finally my turn, they were gone.

I had made the pilgrimage to Medjugorje and I was not going to leave without bringing home rosaries for my friends and family. But by the time my turn came, all of the rosaries were gone.

I tried not to look annoyed but the disappointment and agitation must have been apparent as I walked into the small shop and saw the empty rack with the words Wooden Rosaries on the top. I dragged my feet and tried to look interested in the medals and prayer cards. I felt like a child who had dropped his double scoop of rocky road ice cream, staring at the emptiness and what might have been.

I paced and pouted and told myself that I was acting like a two year old. But my disappointment hung on me like a heavy burden.

Why not ask, I thought. My father had always taught me to ask if I could not find what I wanted. So I did.

But the kind clerk only shook her head.

"Sorry, sir, we sold out of them about thirty minutes ago," she said, frowning.

151

152

I hung my head and turned, only to run into a little old woman carrying five wooden rosaries. She must have noticed my scowl because she instantly said, "Sir, I have extra rosaries. Would you like one?"

I was overjoyed but certainly unprepared for what was to follow. Everywhere I looked strangers were walking up to me and offering their "extras."

Maybe it was a coincidence and maybe just the kindness of strangers, but as I stood in that shop with an armful of wooden rosaries, I am certain that I felt Mother Mary's grace and heard her wisdom. For I left that shop with the knowledge that good things come with time and especially with patience.

Rich M.

153

She struggled slightly for a second, freed herself, and then seemed to float on a cushion of air as she gently emerged from the thorn bush. Her voice was sweet and soft like a child's. Her robe was silver with gold trimming that seemed to sparkle and shimmer as she levitated about six inches from the ground. I waited in anticipation, watching her kind, round face until her lips moved and I heard, "Pray, pray, pray." I waited, paralyzed with fear. No, not fear really, maybe the feeling was more of awe than fear. I waited for more instruction, and I remember feeling that I could wait forever for whatever this elegantly humble person wanted to tell me.

I watched as her small lips formed words and her blue eyes delivered the message:

"The world offers me thorns, but you offer me a way to the world through your prayers." I must have blacked out because the next thing I knew, Father Kendall was holding a cool rag to my forehead. I tried to repeat the words, but as I looked into Father Kendall's glasses, I could not see his eyes. I remember thinking that all I saw was my own reflection—a poor, frightened woman who was losing her senses.

I avoided church for the next few weeks mostly because

I was afraid, but by the third week, I knew that it was time. I struggled through the heavy oaken doors and sullenly made my way to the front of the church. It was Monday morning, and I knew I would be alone, although I wasn't so sure I wanted to be. But I knew that I had to be there—for her. If she had something else to tell me, I wanted to hear it. I had to know.

Before I could even kneel, I felt her. It was the same awe and amazement, yet when I looked at her, this time it was different. The elegance was gone. Her silver and gold robe was now tarnished brown and on her head was a crown of pewter. Instead of floating peacefully, she now appeared sitting on a wooden throne. I didn't understand it and I shuddered, as a tear seemed to roll down her still beautiful face. I prayed for clarity as I heard the same sweet voice: "He has carved this throne from the wood of the cross and this crown from the cup of his passion."

That was thirteen years ago and I suppose I am not so naïve and scared as I was then. I have remained opened to Mary and she has continued to appear and teach and ask for my help. And the message is always the same—Teach the people to be virtuous so they may see the wondrous kingdom of Heaven.

Sylvia G.

I was in a hurry, I was frustrated, the closet was a mess and I just kept trying to get the door to close. "Just close," I thought, "just close." I was in one of those irrational moods where I just wanted to push harder. I didn't stop to see what was blocking the door, I just pushed hoping to hear the door latch but instead I heard a sickening sound . . . and screams. It was my son's fingers that had been blocking the door. Within seconds his two fingers had swollen so much they looked like one, hanging there limp, unusable and already turning purple. They were broken, I was sure of it.

He was crying, I was crying and I was praying and pleading for help as I got out the bottle of Lourdes water. "If anything I've done at the Marian Center means anything to you, help my child," I prayed. "Saint Bernadette, pray for us. Our Lady of Lourdes, pray and help me with my son's fingers."

I put the healing water on the fingers and the water melted the swelling immediately. Within minutes his tiny fingers went from dark purple to pink.

The entire experience couldn't have lasted more than five minutes, but it left me with no doubt about Mary's love or God's presence.

I think that's what she wanted—for me to have no doubts. I had been holding back at the Marian Center, where I worked, thinking, "I'll give you this much time, but I still want to do this for myself. I'm not going to give you all my time, I want to give it in little measures."

But that's not what Mary wants. She wants it all. It was like God just tapped my shoulder with his fingers and said, "You know I'm really here, wake up, there's things I want you to do for me to help me help my Son's mission and to help foster respect and devotion to Mary."

It changed me completely.

John B.

had a mammogram followed by a biopsy. I was scheduled for surgery. I began using Lourdes water on my left breast everyday and prayed. I had surgery and thanks to Our Lady of Lourdes my prayers were answered. The results of the tests were benign.

N.M., Mississippi

N̳ow it was just an ordinary rose. I had been carrying it for several hours, and as I approached the house of Estella Roweesa, I noticed that it was wilted and its sweet scent long gone. Yes, the beautiful red rose that I had so carefully selected from the rosebush that I had planted in St. Paul's Catholic Church grotto was now a pathetic aggregate of withered petals.

Oh, well, I rationalized, I suppose, as the cliché goes, it's the thought that counts.

I knocked hard on the door and to my surprise it opened immediately. I jumped as the hand came out and took the rose. I stood there for what seemed like forever, waiting for the invitation and the greeting, but neither came—only the hand motioning me to follow.

I began to think that it was a mistake in coming to this house. Usually, I would have ignored the invitation, because I never really believed in the apparitions. Don't get me wrong; I am a devout Christian and dedicated follower of the Legion of Mary, but I guess I had never really bought into the idea that she would appear in three dimension and in the twenty-first century.

So, as I was ushered into the worn-out, creaky house, I

realized that maybe it was all a mistake. I shouldn't have come thousands of miles to this little bungalow in Scottsdale, Arizona. It was not for me.

But I continued to follow the hand as it beckoned me to the back of the house and through a screened door that looked like it was hanging on by one tiny hinge. Or maybe it just reminded me that perhaps it was I who was hanging on by one tiny hinge.

And what I remember most about those few seconds was the deafening silence. Was I alone with the hand? Was it all a trick? Could I be losing my sanity?

Shaking off my confusion and doubt, I followed the hand out of the house and into the backyard. And what awaited me there was the most astounding spectacle that I had ever seen.

In the backyard the size of a small classroom stood a mass of people as silent as death. I half expected the dilapidated door to creak as I pushed it open and became one of them. But the door was silent, the throng of humanity was silent, and I too did not utter a sound.

I wedged myself politely between two strangers and turned toward what appeared to be a stage bright with artificial light. After about ten minutes, the shadowy figure

Virgin most powerful

of a woman glided along the platform and stood looking out into the crowd of what must have been at least two hundred people.

"Would the man who brought the rose from St. Paul's please come with me," said the voice.

I stood there in awe, and then my feet seemed to move involuntarily. I followed her through the crowd and into a tiny garage where I saw several people seated at an old, round, weather-beaten table.

"Have a seat," she said. I remember my relief when finally someone was talking to me. I also remember my shock when she told me why I was there.

"I am Estella Roweesa," she said. "And I have a message for you."

Imagine my surprise when she continued, "Our Lady wants you to know that she appreciates all of your hard work in organizing and building the grotto at St. Paul's."

And then again, imagine my surprise when I got back in my car later that night to the overwhelmingly powerful scent of roses that engulfed my tiny green Subaru.

And although I did not witness any apparitions there, Estella Roweesa sure made a believer out of me on that tenth day of April, and what I call fondly now, A Day of the Rose.

Rich M.

161

Since our move to Denver in 1974, and what I have always called "my meeting" with the Blessed Mother, I again have become a successful businessman. But something certainly has changed. I feel a peace that I have never felt before, and I have met the most incredible people, real people who truly know the meaning of life.

In particular, my wife and I have been lucky enough to become friends with Ed and Audrey Jackson, a fabulous couple who moved to Colorado from New York about fifteen years ago. They told us that they felt a calling from the Blessed Mother and decided to purchase land in Colorado. And this is where their story gets really interesting.

When Ed and Audrey were looking for land, they came upon a piece of property in the Sangre de Cristo mountains that had a statue of Mary on it. They told me how they were trying to decide if it was Our Lady of Fatima or Our Lady of Perpetual Help. They concluded that it really didn't matter, saw it as a sign, and decided to purchase the land right away. The most interesting aspect however was that, when they returned to the land after the purchase, the statue was gone. They immediately called the Realtor to ask about the statue. Her response no doubt came as a shock. She told them that she had been familiar with this property for

162

163

decades and that at no time had there been a statue of Mary on it. The Jacksons said that it was then that they knew they had chosen the right place on which to build a retreat for priests. And you can still see this beautiful retreat, better known today as the Sangre de Cristo Church.

I always knew that the Jacksons were special people. And in fact, when Ed died last year, something equally as incredible happened at his funeral. My wife and I were at the gravesite for the funeral and were of course very sad to lose our dear friend. But as the solemn ceremony continued with the presentation of the flag and the honor guard, I looked up at the sky and saw the most unbelievable sight imaginable. There amidst the crystal blue sky were three cloud-like vapors in the shape of angels. I remember being struck by the fact that they were all exactly the same size and all facing west. I nudged my wife and pointed to the sky. I saw her eyes widen and her mouth fall open as she looked first in disbelief at me and then at the sky and then again at me.

Some people say that we see things that we want to see, and maybe that is true. Nevertheless, my wife and I know what we saw that day. And we also know that we have been truly blessed just knowing Ed and Audrey Jackson.

Dick A.

My devotion to Mary, Our Blessed Mother, comes in the form of the "colcha." I am a seamstress for Our Lady. I sew traditional Spanish robes in honor of Mary's dedication to her people.

"Colcha" is a Spanish word for "blanket" that dates back to colonial times. In the 1600s, when a blanket developed a hole in it, women embroidered a flower or bird to fill in the space. This method became a work of art and the alteration became known as the "colcha stitch."

At the same time that I was asked to sew for Our Lady, I met a woman who told me about the Spanish colonial revival art of the "colcha." I immediately asked her to teach this art to me so that I could make a traditional Spanish dress for the Virgin Mary. Monica Sosaya Halford was happy to teach, and I was happy to learn.

And soon I learned that this was no ordinary sewing method. In fact, the making of the traditional colcha was much more complicated than I ever imagined.

First, you actually start by buying fleece that only comes from the "churro sheep"—the Spanish prize sheep of New Mexico. Then, you must spin the fleece, which is called "spinning the grease." Next, you must wash the fleece in yucca root and rainwater to purify it. Then comes the

166

dyeing that involves only natural dyes from New Mexico. For example, you might use wild spinach for green or indigo root for blue. Finally, you are ready to weave. The whole process, as you can see, is very complicated.

When I first decided to try this method I had no idea how time consuming it would be. In fact, the whole process to make one dress took me about a year to complete. But of course, as my mother used to say, great things take time. And indeed when I finished my project and stepped back to look at this amazing robe that I had made, I knew that I could truly call it great.

I have always heard people say, "It is my calling to do this," but I never really believed in such a thing until now. I do believe that Mary, Mother of God, wanted me to learn and to teach. And because of this gift, I now have formed a group that I call "The Women's Project of Santa Fe." I feel fortunate to be able to teach women this method. In fact, we have now started to use our talents in the form of prayer/sewing circles. As we sew beads, ribbons, buttons, etc., and as we weave and dye, we say prayers for people in our community.

Our hope is that the "colcha" is truly serving its purpose and "blanketing" our community with warmth and love.

Julia G.

CHERI LOMONTE
LA CONQUISTADORA (COLCHA MADE BY JULIA GOMEZ)

One day Mary was in her house and suddenly an angel came and said, "Mary, you shall have a baby boy and you will name him Jesus." Then for a while she was frightened. Then she went to Joseph and said, "We better do what is best for us."

Then Joseph said, "It might be better if we go get advice from the innkeeper in Bethlehem. We will leave in the morning."

When morning came, Mary said, "What will we go on, we don't want to walk, do we?"

"Well, we can go on Little Ollie." Mary said, "We can't both fit on him."

Joseph said, "Then I will just walk."

When they started off, Little Ollie looked concerned. Mary got on Little Ollie and Joseph walked by Ollie and steered him. Sixty minutes passed and Ollie's feet were hurt. They were bleeding because they had to walk over lots of spikey stones. When they got to the inn they said, "Are there any rooms?"

The innkeeper said, "I'm afraid not at all. We only have a very old stable."

Mary said, "That will do."

FATHER WILLIAM HART MCNICHOLS
THE HOLY FAMILY

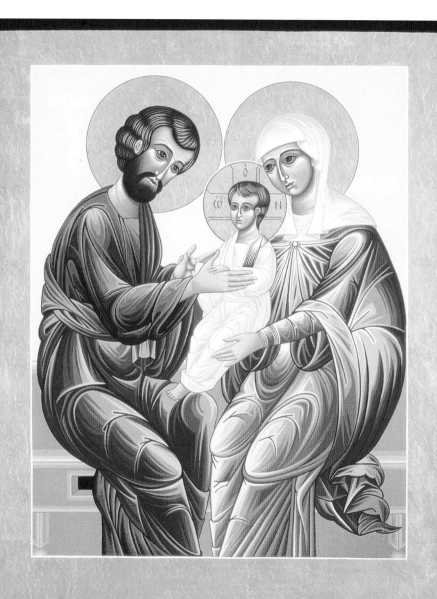

So they went to the stable and Mary said, "Put the manger right here."

Joseph put it right in the middle of the stable, and right in the middle of the animals, too.

It was time for the baby. The baby came and it was beautiful. Mary was very happy and she thought that he was cold so she sent out for swaddling clothes. When Mary got some swaddling clothes she wrapped them around baby Jesus to keep him warm. Baby Jesus was happy too. Three wise men came and gave the baby gold, frankincense, and myrrh. Everyone was happy.

Patrick H.

170

Since November I have had health problems and have been in and out of the hospital several times with mini strokes and heart attacks. I asked Mary to answer my prayers and help me get well. I feel that my prayers have been answered.

R.D., Kansas

f you'd like to go, I'll take you there," smiled my mother as she set the book down on the coffee table.

My mother is a very organized, rational person who has planned every detail of her life. She does not do or say things impetuously, so I was quite surprised when she offered to take me to Medjugorje on what seemed like a whim.

"Mom, are you serious?" I asked hesitantly.

"Absolutely," she nodded. "I'll plan it all."

And I knew she would.

On May 5, 2002, my mother and I set out on our pilgrimage to Medjugorje. Neither of us knew much about the place, except about the apparitions of Mary, of course. And we both have a strong belief in our faith and the power of the Holy Spirit and the Virgin Mary.

But we are also rational human beings with little faith in the supernatural. So needless to say, we didn't know what we were in for on that fifth day of May.

On our arrival, we were surprised to find that though our accommodations were sparse, we both talked immediately about the sense of peace that we felt there. It was, as I say, a feeling, but one that can only be described as

quiet, serene, and calming.

As we unpacked, we noticed that the sun was as bright as we had ever seen it. We noticed too how it lit up our room as we both reached for our sunglasses at the same time.

We were just getting ready to wash up so we could go out and see the sights, when someone knocked on our door.

The beautiful, Norwegian-looking woman didn't bother introducing herself but instead grabbed my hand and spoke excitedly, "Come now, please, the miracle, it is happening."

My mother and I were both ready for anything; after all, we had made the journey to the other side of the world. But we were certainly not prepared for what we saw.

The sun's rays seemed to form a circle around us, each ray a purple hue mixed with milky white tones. The sun itself, oddly enough, was easy to look at and seemed to have some filter blocking its intense heat and glare. Then the edges of the rays began to lengthen until they encircled us with purple and white stripes. And then the most amazing sight of all—the purple and white colors combined to form a deep purple cloud that then vanished into the heavens.

My mother and I often talk about our experience at Medjugorje and although we are not artists, we both have

173

tried, over and over, to sketch the amazing event—but to no avail.

We have finally decided just to remember the sight in our minds and to feel it in our hearts, for we truly believe that we witnessed what some people call the Miracle of the Sun.

Siobhan L.

My husband Moe suffered several strokes in December and was not able to eat. He ate pureed foods and still kept choking. He also had pneumonia a number of times. By April he was choking so bad the doctors put a feeding tube in his stomach and he had to eat through a tube. I never gave up, but had to put Moe in a nursing home in May. I sent for Lourdes water and began using it on him by putting the Lourdes water in his drink and applesauce when they tried to feed him by mouth. Moe got better and is now eating three meals a day. I felt a miracle had happened. When he left the Veteran's Administration hospital in Loma Linda, California, the doctor did not give him much hope for the future. Today Moe walks with a walker and eats three meals a day. Thank you, Mary.

R.A., California

When I lived in Florida, I served as the sacristan at St. John's Church. It was wonderful being so close to the Eucharist, to Jesus and the sacraments, and to work with the many Eucharistic ministers. It was an incredible time of my life.

One special event that was particularly beautiful was the crowning in May of Mary's statue. The eighth grade boys and girls from the associated school filed through the church with one of the girls chosen to place the crown on Mary. This was doubly exciting for me because I had children in this school and a son who was in the eighth-grade class.

For this event, I had purchased a beautiful crown of flowers to place on Mary's statue. I took it to the school and gave it to the principal, saying, "This is for Rachel." She was the one chosen to crown Mary. I then ran back to church to prepare for the children's mass.

Everything was beautiful. The altar was set up and the children came walking down the aisle—the girls dressed in their beautiful white dresses, and the boys in their suits. When they walked into the church, Rachel had the crown of flowers—on her own head. I thought "Oh my gosh! Did someone misunderstand? I gave this to the principal and those were for Mary!" I looked at Mary's statue and said, "I am so sorry. This isn't what I planned."

Then it was as though Mary smiled and said to me, "I have my crown, don't you worry. Let this be. Let this young girl have this beautiful crown." I immediately felt comforted and calmly watched as Rachel put a small crown of plastic flowers on Mary's head.

A week later, Rachel's dad came running into the Sacristy with pictures. In the pictures it showed Rachel crowning Mary, and with the way the light shown, the crown of plastic flowers looked like a crown of real gold! It was incredible! The picture was magnificent. That confirmed for me as much as anything that what Mary had told me was true, she had her crown and wanted one young girl for a day to know some of her beauty.

Carolyn Rae F.

had heard about the appearances of Our Lady Queen of Peace, but I had never really thought much about them until I met Maria, a dark little woman with a big kind face. She told me that she was hosting a trip to Medjugorje, and I told her that I was thinking about selling the dress and ring, since I had recently called off the wedding, and perhaps I could use the money for a trip to see the Blessed Virgin. I remember distinctly that she smiled, revealing her conspicuously crooked teeth, gave me a strange look, shook her wide, curly hair, and said, "Oh, there will be no need for that." Not until a few years later did I realize what she had meant on that day back in 1987.

Over the next few years, I started attending church regularly and even tried my hand at playing guitar and then songwriting. One composition in particular caught the attention of my friend, who was a member of the church choir at the time. She asked me to play it for the choir and, to my surprise, they loved it. In fact, they immediately asked me to play my "Hymn to Mary" for a church event—some small gathering, or so I thought.

It turned out that I was to perform in front of eight hundred people while a specialist on Medjugorje—Tom

178

Hurlington—spoke about the apparitions of Mary. I recall thinking that there was no way on earth that I could perform with eight hundred pairs of eyes and eight hundred pairs of ears focused on me.

I also recall the calm that pervaded my senses as I stepped up to the microphone. It was the most exhilarating feeling I had ever felt in my young life. As I returned to my seat, my soul was ten feet off the ground, Mr. Hurlington continued by asking the crowd to submit questions that would be randomly read and answered. I watched his long, thin face, thinking about how much time he must have spent researching the Blessed Mother, when I heard my name. "There seems to be a question addressed to Sylvia," the voice seemed to say. Was I dreaming? Yes, that is my name, but I certainly did not think it was addressed to me! My previous calm turned to fluster as he read: "Dear Sylvia, Our company would like to know if we could host your trip to Medjugorje."

That was 1989 and until this day, I do not know who or how, and yet I must truly believe that Mary played some kind of role in my memorable trip to Medjugorje. And who would have known that in fact there would be "no need for that," as Maria had told me several years before.

Sylvia G.

179

y name is Mary and I grew up being repeatedly reminded by my mother that when I was born, she consecrated me to the Blessed Mother. She always told me to be good and to be always mindful that I was named after Mary, Mother of God. I guess I considered myself special or rather, felt I had a special connection to Mary because of my mother's constant reminders. But it was not until I was a grown woman that I was truly able to experience that special bond with Our Lady.

It all started when my family moved to a new parish, and we started attending St. Francis of Assisi. I had always paid attention to statues of Mary, but this church in particular was unique in the colorful clothing that adorned the Blessed Mother.

One particular Sunday as I knelt and admired the clothing, I began to think that it would be such an honor to sew for the Virgin Mother. It was the first Sunday of the month and that meant donut day. My children knew it was "donut Sunday," so there was no way of escaping without first visiting the Frisatti room. As my children rushed off to be the first in line for the sweet, sugary treats, a woman whom I had never seen before came up to me and

introduced herself.

"Oh, yes, you're Mary, right?" she said. Before I could ask how she knew my name, she said, "And I hear that you are a seamstress." Again I was shocked but could not get a word in edgewise.

"My name is Laura Grady," she said. "I am in charge of the seamstresses for the Blessed Mother. In fact, I need someone who can sew her Fiesta Vestment. Would you be interested, Mary?"

"It would be an honor," the words flew from my mouth.

And that day I knew that Mary really had chosen me. Since then, I have sewn over three hundred dresses for the Blessed Mother. And I will continue to sew for Our Lady for as long as she wills it and as long as I am able.

Mary D.

183

During the year 2002, I began to notice a growing discomfort in my knees. I chose not to take anything for the pain or seek the help of a doctor. I know so many people who complain of arthritis and who cannot go on with their daily tasks because they hurt. I didn't want to be that way. When I mentioned the discomfort to my sister, she immediately said, "It's probably arthritis." I emphatically replied, "No, I don't have arthritis!" I didn't want to have that disease and I refused to own it.

184

However, as time went on the pain became more severe. I knew I had to do something to relieve the pain so each time I sat down I would put my hands on my knees and say, "I am healed. I am healed. I am healed." I repeated this positive phrase over and over. It didn't work. By the end of November, the pain was so intense it was difficult to sleep at night.

On December 8, we had a "Mother Mary Energy Day." This was a day of prayer and thanksgiving similar to others we had held since 1999. During that time, many people had been healed, both physically and emotionally, thanks to the intercessions of Holy Mother Mary. On that afternoon, my husband Bob and I went in the backyard at our home in

Florida, where we prayed the rosary and sang songs to Mary. We scanned the skies for manifestations of her love, but did not see anything as we had on some of the previous "Energy Days."

The rest of the day was fairly typical. We took a nap, ate dinner, watched TV. I was working on a pine-cone wreath and when I stood up, I noticed it was easier for me to stand and walk. When I woke up the next morning, I noticed that I had slept really, really well without any pain.

Then the realization of what had happened came to me! I grabbed Bob and was dancing around, shouting, "I've been healed! I've been healed!" I immediately gave thanks to our Holy Mother.

I have been free of pain ever since. Now I can kneel and pray.

Mary H.

People often ask me how I got started sewing dresses for the Virgin Mary. My answer is always, "I don't know." I guess my grandmother had some influence on me, since she was a seamstress and I spent a great deal of my youth with her. But I always felt that there was something more—perhaps something that reverberated in my soul since I was nine when my grandfather took me to see the Fiesta Queen. It seems like that is the first time I can truly remember the feeling of excitement, of intense emotions, of spiritual bliss, if there is such a thing. And that is also the time that I knew I wanted to make dresses for Our Lady.

I also knew that I wanted to make unique dresses to honor Our Blessed Mother. I had this idea early on that perhaps my designs could symbolize religious events. I started with a dress that included the Rose of Sharon, which of course is the foretelling of Mary in the Old Testament. The next dress I made included the symbolism of the number three—the three ages of man and the Holy Trinity. I recently completed a dress using bright orange and yellow fabric to represent the burning bush. My next dress will include a representation of the twelve apostles, which I hope to finish next month.

CHERI LOMONTE
IMMACULATE HEART OF MARY

I suppose my dresses are also unique because of my method of sewing. As I sew, I pray for the souls in Purgatory. For example, each bead, each button, and each stitch might represent a person that needs Our Blessed Mother's intervention in order to ascend into Heaven. And at the end of each sewing session, I always end with the same prayer: "Mother, keep us in your arms and out of despair."

Today I am celebrating my twenty-third birthday. Many people look at me in disbelief when I tell them that I sewed my first dress for the Blessed Mother when I was fifteen years old. They have a difficult time believing my age when I explain the symbolism of the designs in my dresses. And I often hear, "You must be so proud of yourself." But I always tell them that it is not about pride at all. In fact, it is a very humbling experience to sew for Our Lady. Some people like to say that it is my calling, but whatever it is, I truly feel honored and blessed to have such an intimate relationship with the Mother of God.

Paul V.

We all know about life's forks in the road. We all know how one door opens as another closes. As humans, I suppose we expect rough times in our lives. But I really had not experienced failure, and when I did, believe me, I was not prepared. I did not expect the door to close and close and close.

My name is Dick, and I suppose I have a story to tell. Prior to 1974, I was a very successful businessman in Kansas City. I had all the money I wanted, a thriving business, a wonderful wife, and four beautiful daughters. Life was good. Nothing could go wrong, or so I thought.

I had been working on a very large oil deal that I thought was a sure thing. It was going to mean that we could finally buy that huge house that we had been eyeing for months. My wife had even investigated the new neighborhood's schools—the best in Kansas City, of course. But life has a way of taking its own path. I got the call just as I was getting ready to head home for the weekend. I couldn't believe my ears—the whole deal was off. Everything seemed to fall apart as I heard the words: "Dick, it's over. They've changed their minds. No go. And by the way, we probably won't be renewing your contract."

How would I tell my wife? My children? How could I have failed? This had never happened to me before. I was devastated.

But the next few months were even more devastating. Our stocks plummeted, and we realized that we would have to sell our house to relieve some of our debt. And to top it all off, I found out that I had serious heart problems.

That was when we decided to move to Colorado. My family had always loved the beauty of Colorado and, although I did not have a job, we took the plunge. My family was excited, but I was nervous. What was I doing moving without a job? Had I lost my mind? Was this the right decision?

It was 1974, and it was the beginning of my real life, my spiritual life, that is. And it was the beginning of my meetings with Our Lady. I should tell you right away that I have not actually had visions, nor have I directly communicated with Mary, the Blessed Mother, but things have happened to me that deserve telling…things that have changed my life.

A few months after we arrived in Denver I decided to visit the Mother Cabrini Shrine in Golden, Colorado. A friend of mine had told me that I needed to see the view of

Denver from the shrine. He also had told me about a woman named Teresa Lopez, who had been receiving messages there from Our Blessed Mother. He had even shown me a newspaper article with a picture of this beautiful, dark-eyed woman with unusually shiny black hair. I was curious but not particularly so. I guess I didn't think too much of it at the time. But I was excited about seeing the shrine, because I felt like I needed to start praying again. I had to get back on my feet, and I had to know if I had made the right decision in moving to Denver. I decided to pray to Our Mother and ask for her guidance and help in my new endeavors in Denver.

I suppose I chose an odd day for my first visit because that particular weekend there had been a huge snowstorm in Denver. As I made my way up the stairs of the shrine, I noticed the drifting snow on the walkway and soon realized that people were walking towards me with shovels. Of course it made sense to help, so even before I reached the statue, someone handed me a shovel. I remember thinking that it was a strange, yet beautiful scene—people lined up shoveling in silence. Then I noticed her on the walkway below. It couldn't be, or could it? The dark eyes, the shiny black hair…

And before I knew it, she looked up, right at me, and exclaimed, "Oh my goodness, look at this." I jumped, immediately dropped my shovel, and made my way to her. "Look at this," she said again. I looked in the snow and saw it. She had uncovered an unusual blue streak in the snow. It seemed to be a perfect arc of some sort, about six inches wide and three feet in length. I was taken aback because of the perfection of the arc and the way the powdery blue color shimmered in the snow. I introduced myself to her and soon realized that I was right…it was her, Teresa Lopez. No sooner had I gone back to shoveling when I heard it again: "Oh, another one, come and look at this one, Dick." I was shocked to see the same arc, but this one was a deep, scarlet red…a blood red perhaps. It didn't shine as the blue had but instead lay there like a weight upon the once feathery snow. This time I had to investigate.

I could feel her eyes on my back as I knelt to get a closer look. I wondered why she wasn't doing the same. But as I reached out to touch the arc, I had this weird sensation in my arm. It was almost like a shooting pain, a stinging in my wrist. I jerked back, and turned to look at her, but she was gone. I looked around, no one. I climbed up the stairs and then down. People looked at me like I was crazy. A petite, blonde woman must have noticed my exasperation because she touched my arm and asked if I needed help. I looked at her wide blue eyes, composed myself, and said, "I think I just got it, thank you." I put down my shovel, walked back to my car, and felt an overwhelming calm—the calm that so many people have described when they have had a chance meeting with the Blessed Mother.

All the way home I remember repeating the word "powerful" in my head. And all I could think of was the excitement inside as I rushed home to tell my wife about my experience. To my surprise, however, she was waiting on the porch for me with a smile as big as Texas. "You'll never believe who called, honey, Joe Linderman. Yes, Mr. Linderman wants you to call right away. He said he has some work that you might be interested in and wants you to attend an important meeting on Tuesday," she blurted.

Two important meetings in one week, I thought. I smiled and knew that everything would be O.K. And believe me, it's been far better than O.K.—it's been a dream. And everyday I thank Mary, the Blessed Mother, for all of my successes.

Richard A.

I suppose I should have been a bit more concerned with my appearance—no makeup to hide the puffy eyes, no barrette to pull back the bushy hair—but after all, it was 2:25 a.m. The policeman didn't seem to mind, though, as he kindly asked me to try to remember the exact contents of my purse.

License, Visa, MasterCard, gift certificates to Nordstrom's and the Gap, checkbook, all things replaceable, I thought. And then I remembered the $300 in cash that my sister had given to me as a gift—"just because," she had told me. Looking back, I suppose I hadn't spent it because maybe I felt like I was carrying around a piece of her with me for three months.

"O Mary, sweet Mother of God," I silently prayed, "Please let me get my purse back." I always prayed to Mary when I was feeling desperate. And I was certainly feeling desperate now.

"It's my own fault," I told Officer MacDonald. "For one, I never should have left my purse in the car, and for two, I should have checked to make sure that my garage door was closed before going to bed. Carelessness, that's all," I admitted and thanked him for coming.

194

Waking up to the news that someone had been in my garage and in my car, going through my personal things and then taking my purse, was alarming to say the least. As I fell into my big soft velvet chair, I felt violated and angry, but most of all helpless. My stomach muscles began to cramp and my throat began to tighten. I reached for the soft blanket and covered my cold feet. "Got to get some rest," I thought. "Lots to do tomorrow…."

"Mom, I'm hungry," came the words from a far-off land. "Mom, get up, I want some breakfast," came the voice again. I must have jumped three feet in the air when I realized that I had fallen into what must have been a deep sleep. "Oh, no, 7:15, got to make breakfast, got to get the kids off to school, got to get to work…. got to get a new license, got to cancel bank accounts," I thought.

I turned on the morning news on TV and the first thing I saw was the beautiful little three-year-old girl. Her big brown eyes and coal black hair made her look like a little princess from the Middle East.

"…Three year old abducted last night by an intruder into a Lakewood home…desperate parents are requesting any information that might lead to their daughter," the newscaster continued.

"How frightening," I thought. "How bold, how dare someone come in and take their baby!" I thought of my purse and my intruder and realized how unimportant my stolen purse was now.

"Oh Blessed Mother," I prayed as tears began to form. "I have been so selfish and petty. How could I think that paper and cards and money were of any importance whatsoever. Please, Mother of God, please return that beautiful girl to her poor, helpless parents. I don't care about a stupid purse."

And I went on with my day.

Looking back, Monday was actually a great day. Work had gone well and I felt happy, even after the events of the night before.

After work, the soccer carpool, and the grocery store, I arrived home and began to prepare dinner. I switched on the TV and to my surprise, the first thing that appeared was that beautiful little brown-eyed princess. The sound was muted so I immediately grabbed for the remote. Oh no, I remembered, the abducted girl. But the newscaster was smiling. Could it be good news?

"At 2:25 today, police found Grace Blesloe, the three-year-old girl who was abducted from her home on 19th and Jewell in Lakewood last night. She was found by a Good

197

Samaritan at a bus stop in downtown Denver, crying and cold, but unharmed. She has been returned safely to her frantic parents."

I began to cry and immediately thanked Mary for answering my prayers.

And if one miracle was not enough, about thirty minutes later, as I was putting the spaghetti on the table, the phone rang.

"Ms. Hanks?" said the voice. "Are you Annette Hanks on 244 Amaranth St. in Aurora?"

"Yes, this is Annette Hanks," I answered. "Can I help you?"

"I just wanted to let you know that I found your purse at our place of business and have it here, if you would like to come and pick it up."

I couldn't believe my ears. It couldn't be.

"I am Timmy Franklin," the good-looking young man said when we arrived at his business. He smiled and handed me my purse. "I found it on the sidewalk outside and called you immediately. I had my wallet stolen once right out of my pocket, in fact. I know how frustrating that can be."

Timmy Franklin could not have been more than twenty. He was amiable and kind and I could tell he was quite the talker. I listened, keeping my eyes on him so as not to be rude, and felt around in my purse.

"It couldn't be," I thought. "No way could the intruder have missed it." But as I pulled out the white and red bank envelope, I knew that it was real. The $300 cash was still there—the money from my sister—the three crisp $100 bills were in place.

And then I knew exactly what I had to do. I pulled out the money and offered it to Timmy Franklin.

"Your reward," I said.

But Timmy Franklin would hear of no such thing. "I just hope someone does the same for me one day, if I need," he smiled.

"Another Good Samaritan," I thought as I headed home.

And another miracle on what has been a truly amazing day.

Annette H.

had been to Medjugorje several times, and I had heard several accounts of people witnessing miracles. But I had not experienced one myself, until that day I had to speak at the Fatima Retreat.

I had a lot of information to share and stories to tell, and that is why Father Michael had asked me to speak to the congregation. But for some reason, I was afraid. I was afraid to speak in front of two hundred people. And I was afraid that I would disappoint them.

But I knew that I had to do it. Father Michael was counting on me.

So I said a prayer to Mary, the Blessed Mother, and I walked up to the microphone with my rosary in my hand. But as I reached for the mike, I felt a presence—a large presence. It felt like people were crowding me, or touching me—like one person was on my left and one on my right. I can honestly say that it was the most unusual sensation that I had ever felt.

I looked to my left and then to my right, but nothing was there. And then I looked out into the crowd and saw a sea of faces, all anticipating my wisdom.

I began to speak and when I did, I felt a nudge, like

someone had poked me in the side. And then I realized that I had not turned on the microphone.

After my speech, I walked off of the podium feeling pretty good. I had remembered everything and had held the attention of the crowd for thirty minutes. I recall thinking how silly I had been to be nervous and how silly I had been to think that people were crowding me.

But when I got to my seat, my seven-year-old son, Kevin, looked oddly at me and asked, "Dad, who were those big men that were standing next to you up there?"

"What are you talking about, son?" I whispered.

"Those huge guys with white stuff coming from their backs—they were so close to you, Dad."

"I thought they looked like big angels or something," he added.

I told him to hush and we'd talk about it later.

But we never did talk about it later. Because later that evening when I asked Kevin about the big men standing next to me, he just looked at me like I was crazy. He had no idea what I was talking about. He had no idea that he had seen big men holding me up as I gave my speech. He had no idea that he had seen angels who had helped me to deliver my message from Medjugorje.

David F.

In Our Lady's garden she stands and waits for you,
The fragrant wind blows softly stirring blossoms in
the air, trees respond and then a suspended hush abides.
In the golden silence you know, She's there.

In this place her gentle spirit touches and sets you free
Talk to her as children would, beseech her loving care
Blend your heart with Hers, plead for all your needs.
Heaven's perfected Love will dispel your darkest fears.

Her arms extend lovingly beckoning every care,
Promise and hope are sustained by God's own hand.
Come into the garden, this holy place of prayer,
Tender is the message, as She intercedes for every prayer.

A Lady, with so many names, She sends your prayers
to God. They rise swiftly on angel's wings then
God plants seeds of hope in your heart.
Sustained now by faith, your journey radiates with hope.

She waits within a garden, a place filled with peace and love.
She's Wisdom's fullest grace, expectantly awaiting all
who dare to come. Remember, God esteems our Mother
as he placed her to reflect the many seasons.

She is perfected love, tender and sublime, keeping
all God's promises She knows, written in Her heart.
She waits to impart Her Love to you. Now, She beckons,
"Come into my garden, I have flowers here for you."

Diane C.

DIANE COOLIDGE
GARDEN

Queen of heavenly peace, brightest morning star, evident in beauty, hear our vision's call. Lady of the fountain's blessing. Holy Scepter guide us. Mother of Eternal God may heaven's thrones be defined today with your unending Love.

Our Lady in the garden, crowned with flower's dew, sits on Angel's shoulders letting life renew. In the stillness listen as Her heart will open doors for you. Every breath She breathes has meaning just for you. Keep her Love radiating in your heart to abide forever.

How God does love His Mother, no doubt within my mind? Set on Wisdom's course, Her counsel bears us on. Thank you for Love's highest gift, separated only by a veil. She is knowledge gathered in a single moment. Stay within Her heart's attentive, adoring gaze.

She is our aspiring hope rising like a dove. Her light streams forth this day. Call upon Her as your Mother and She will answer you. Swiftly her Angels go upon their course, delivering heaven's gifts from cloistered walls above. God's graces flowing down to you, on wings of perfect Love.

She is beauty set in golden raiment, like glistening golden stars. A Mother who keeps provisions for all Her children's rights. A love benign with glory, stretching forth a path for you. Pray with Her each morning and in every hour she will guide and walk with you.

She walks at our side, like a mother who sees Her child to school. Her lessons fill the day. Why would I care to wander from such a quiet place of peace? Eternal is the soul I seek, Come O Mother, and set the skies ablaze with your heavenly fire and free all souls to love this day.

Diane C.

Our Lady, Queen of Peace, whose heart weeps tears of blood for lost souls, we give thee our hearts—change them, transform them, and make them pure. Reform our lives. Protect and console us in our temptations.

Through the most Holy Rosary, we dedicate ourselves to you. Pray with us. Through prayer and fasting, help us to develop a lively conscience, a strong faith, and an inner peace.

Teach us to love, to pray from the heart with love, and to carry our cross for the glory of the Lord. My Mother, we pray that those in the world who do not know you will come to feel your warm embrace, accept your love, and take refuge in your Immaculate Heart. May our hearts be united unto thee, as your heart is united to the Lord of all hearts.

205

Help us to live your message, to understand and accept God's love and peace—to live it and spread it, to be a light borne to those who live in darkness. May we go forth as instruments of peace, instruments of hope, and instruments of joy and, in doing so, oh loving Mother, turn your tears of sorrow into tears of joy.

Amen

Rich M.

206

maybe I can hold
palm cup flights
of light and wonder
release to downwind suns
on wither paths
cotton parachutes of reed-mace
hail Mary
full of grace

wind sown graduating bloom
vine remains in wood
song bird sway
and sing atop a cattail
red wing blackbird and Austrian pea
catch a cloud of spring
the Lord
is with Thee

in july
river otter sleek back
breaks surface
apogee and rings of bright water
constellations and clusters
of great things mean
blessed art thou
amongst women

continued

lanceolate leaves
and marsh pennyworth
colonnades of cypress trees
autumn jellies of vegetation
esters and complicated scents
diaphanous harvest dimplings
and blessed is the fruit
of thy womb Jesus

conceive of flesh
in perfect faith
welcome lord
to the human race
wrought in women
wrought in ark
holy Mary
mother of God

earth cries for rain
first dawn fire
stains the evening dusk
robe of sleep
shallowness of breath
pray for us sinners
now and at the hour of our death

amen

John O.

· ACKNOWLEDGMENTS ·

As I start out "making the most out of the rest of my life," I am reminded that man doesn't do much by himself. And I am no exception.

Thank you, Tony, my dear husband, for your support while we collected stories, drove to Timbuktu and back, dropped everything we were doing to record a story. Thank you for showing me what a partner really does for the other person.

Thank you, Gael, Annette, Brian, Cristian, Father Bill, Bob and Jim. It was so very exciting working with you. Also, I want to thank Barbara Munson and Marjory McNichols Wilson.

Thank you, Patty Sue and Sarah, for your support. You are always there for me.

Thank you to my children, Brennan and Sally, Gabe and Adrienne, Patrick, Kirstin and Tony, Braden, and Brent and Tina.

Thank you, Mother Mary. Thank you for choosing me to tell your stories. I am making the most out of the rest of my life.

CHERI LOMONTE　　AUTHOR/PHOTOGRAPHER

Cheri is a photographer, educator and collector of stories. An accomplished public speaker, Cheri is known for her insights, her creativity and her ability to make connections. She embodies the archetype of the entrepreneur and her soul is nurtured by her family. Her passion is taking photographs and collecting stories of Mother Mary.

GAEL D. HANCOCK　　WRITER/EDITOR

Gael has 25 years of experience in advertising, marketing and public relations. She writes for local and national publications and has completed several children's books. Gael also is a successful fundraiser and is a project development consultant, working with communities and organizations throughout the country. She is second vice president of the Labyrinth Society (www.LabyrinthSociety.org) and is active in her church and community. She lives in Las Vegas with her husband, two children, a golden retriever and, for the time being, her mother-in-law.

ANNETTE HANKS　　TEACHER/WRITER

Annette Hanks Cladny is a writer who lives in Littleton, Colorado with her husband, Mark, and their three children. She has a M.A. in English Literature from the University of Colorado in Boulder and has taught high school English for 21 years. She is presently working on publishing her first novel, *Flights of Angels*, as well as writing her second book, *Driving Me Crazy*. As for the experience of listening to over seventy tape recorded narratives and of putting these accounts into story form, she says that every single story has inspired her on a very spiritual level and has confirmed her faith in the goodness and healing power of Mary.

FATHER WILLIAM HART McNICHOLS　　ARTIST

Born in Denver, Colorado, Father McNichols was ordained a Roman Catholic priest in 1979. In 1983 he received a Master of Fine Arts from Pratt Institute in New York. He moved to New Mexico to study icon painting with the Russian-American master, Robert Lentz. Father McNichols lives in Talpa, New Mexico, where he continues his work with icons and assists Father Martinez at the San Francisco de Asis Church. The artist representative is Debra De la Torre and can be reached at Debra@TaosTraditions.com.

CRISTIAN WHITNEY　　ARTIST

Cristian is the artist of many popular and controversial art shows, such as "I See Red" and "American Freak Show." He is a deeply spiritual man who created the "Mary" collection in this book to express his love and gratitude to the Virgin Mary. All of his collections have been huge successes in his hometown and he is beginning to gain notice around the nation. Whitney lives in Denver with his wife Shari and son Liam. For more information, visit www.THE-77.com.

BRIAN CANTRELL　　BOOK DESIGN

Brian has experience in writing and design, and carries a genuine interest in the visual execution of the creative thought process. He currently resides in Austin, Texas with his wife Amberlee. Please direct any inquiries to briancntrll@aol.com.

Do you have a story about Mary?

I invite you to share with others your prayers, poems, and stories of intercessory miracles.

Send your submissions to me for inclusion in the next edition of *The Healing Touch of Mary*.

Email me at <u>Stories@divineimpressions.com</u>

If you have questions, or would like to *tell* me your story, call me at (800) 682 1729.

All net proceeds from the books will be given to charities.

Thank you,
Cheri Lomonte

· HOW TO ORDER ·

To order a copy or copies of *THE HEALING TOUCH OF MARY*,
WRITE OR CALL:

DIVINE IMPRESSIONS
27 Long Spur
Littleton, CO 80127
800.682.1729
www.divineimpressions.com

Art & Photography Credits

· NOTES ·

· NOTES ·